NEW

AND

IMPROVED

NEW
AND IMPROVED

JAMES LONG

VICTOR BOOKS™
A DIVISION OF SCRIPTURE PRESS PUBLICATIONS INC.
USA CANADA ENGLAND

Second printing, 1986

Bible quotations are from the *New International Version*, © 1978 by the New York International Bible Society. Used by permission.

Library of Congress Catalog Card Number: 82-62437
ISBN: 0-88207-590-X

© 1983, SP Publications, Inc. All rights reserved.
Printed in the United States of America.

VICTOR BOOKS
A division of SP Publications, Inc.
P.O. Box 1825 • Wheaton, Ill. 60187

DEDICATION

Thank You, Lord,
for my son George Michael,
and for his young understanding
of Your better Way!

CONTENTS

1. **Son of Thunder, Son of Love** 13
   1 John 1:1-4

2. **God Is Light, Walk in Light** 25
   1 John 1:5–2:2

3. **Old Commandment, New Commandment** 37
   1 John 2:3-11

4. **New Life, New Peril** 49
   1 John 2:12-17

5. **In the Church, In the Truth** 61
   1 John 2:18-27

6. **Child of God, Child of Satan** 73
   1 John 2:28–3:10

7. **Love in Truth, Love in Action** 85
   1 John 3:11-24

8. **Spirit of Truth, Spirit of Error** 97
   1 John 4:1-6

9. **Live in Love, Live in God** 109
   1 John 4:7-21

10. **Eternal Life, Eternal Son** 121
    1 John 5:1-12

11. **God Hears, God Answers** 133
    1 John 5:13-21

This book is designed for your personal reading pleasure and profit. It is also designed for group study. A leader's guide, with visual aids (SonPower Multiuse Transparency Masters) and Rip-Offs (student activity booklets) are available from your local Christian bookstore or from the publisher.

Thanks, as always, to my wife Harriet
  . . . for loving unselfishly
  . . . for sharing in my work
  . . . for living John's letter

Discovery.
There's a certain brand of
enthusiasm reserved for
people who find things out
and are glad.
  Big things.
  Significant things.
  Hard-to-explain things.

ONE

SON OF THUNDER, SON OF LOVE

1 John 1:1-4

There were a lot of things I could have said—complaints which could have rolled off my mind almost subconsciously. Instead, I listened.

"One person, who really believed God, could turn this city upside down!"

Five minutes earlier we had been laughing about some dumb joke. But the mood had shifted. Now I looked at this man I so greatly respected (nearly old enough to be my dad) and the protests I might have raised seemed insignificant.

Believe God?

God, I might have argued, didn't have to listen to my parents fight.... Could any rational person believe God when He's so utterly remote? ... And did He really *want* our town inverted—right-side-up, upside down?

But even as I stood there in the church parking lot,

listening, I marveled at how I had changed over the past year. Before, I could hardly imagine myself enjoying a conversation with a preacher, much less consider him a friend. Now I knew my defenses had slipped. When he said, "One person, who really believed God, could turn this city upside down," I realized I wanted to be that one person.

But if you have been the typical rowdy type, how do you explain the change in your actions? If your parents have sweated over your rebelliousness, if your teachers have jotted cryptic reports about your misbehavior, and *then* the change comes, how do you tell people, believably, without losing face? Worse yet, if you have a reputation for being wild, how do you change without your friends concluding you've become too strange to associate with?

On the other hand, if my preacher friend is right, if Christianity is true, and if you really believe God, can anything *keep* you from "turning the world upside down"? I had discovered something—something significant, something that had to be shared:

God can make life better.

Seen, Heard, Share the Word

Almost 60 years after the bloody execution of Jesus, after fierce persecution had wracked the early Christians, an old man sat down to write a letter. He wanted the letter to be an encouragement. He wanted it to be a warning. And he wanted that letter to be a reminder—a backward glance at the pivotal point of history.

It couldn't be cold or impersonal; Christianity is neither. It couldn't be stuffy or bookish; God isn't like that. This letter had to be warm, even tender. And it had to center on a dead man, more than man, and now living. That letter, 1 John, was to be a crucial reminder of a significant, yet hard to explain, discovery.

John began simply, "That which was from the beginning, which we have heard, which we have seen with our eyes, which we have looked at and our hands have touched—this we proclaim concerning the Word of life" (1 John 1:1).

We have heard.
We have seen with our eyes.
We have looked at.
Our hands have touched.

The personal quality is unmistakable. And the next two verses underscore the same mood:

We have seen it and testify to it.
We have seen and heard.

John wanted it clear, Christianity is not built on a cute collection of human ideas. It is linked to a Person, a Person John had encountered face to face. And as John writes, it seems he flashes back six decades to retrace his own encounter with Jesus Christ, and his own unshakable conclusion:

God can make life better.

To Net a Fisherman

Sweating under a hot white sun, two sets of brothers labored together in a common trade—Simon (later called Peter) and his brother Andrew; James and his younger brother John. They spent their days tugging at nets often as long as 300 feet, stretched between two boats, or casting smaller nets single-handedly. But one day as the brothers were mending their nets, Jesus walked along the shore. He came first to Simon and Andrew and then to James and John. His invitation: "Come, follow Me ... and I will make you fishers of men" (Mark 1:17).

This was not John's first encounter with Jesus. John had met the Carpenter from Nazareth on a previous occasion (John 1:29-42). But this time, the fisherman and his friends dropped their nets and followed.

A close relationship developed between Jesus and the brothers, especially Peter, James, and John. John was with Jesus when He raised Jairus' daughter from the dead (Mark 5:37). John watched the 12-year-old, obviously dead, respond to Jesus' words, "Get up!"

John was with Jesus when His appearance suddenly changed, when He was "transfigured." "His clothes became dazzling white, whiter than anyone in the world could bleach them. And there appeared before them Elijah and Moses, who were talking with Jesus" (Mark 9:2-3).

John was with Jesus in the Garden of Gethsemane the night Jesus was arrested. John heard Jesus that night, and saw His distress. "My soul is overwhelmed with sorrow to the point of death," Jesus had said (Mark 14:34).

John was the only disciple at the crucifixion of Jesus, where Jesus committed His mother into John's care (John 19:26-27). And John was the first of the disciples to see the empty grave and believe in the Resurrection (John 20:8). Following Jesus' return to heaven, John became a key leader in the Jerusalem church. He was present when the lame man was healed. And with Peter, John was hauled before the Jewish leaders and rebuked for preaching about Jesus (Acts 3–4). Later, John met with the Apostle Paul following his conversion to Christianity (Galatians 2:9).

John had heard Jesus, had seen Him with his eyes, had touched Him. So when he wrote 1 John, he wrote from a backlog of unforgettable memories.

"The life appeared; we have seen it and testify to it, and we proclaim to you the eternal life, which was with the Father and has appeared to us" (1 John 1:2).

But there was another dimension to John's recollections:

"Call Down Fire!"

Tucked away in Mark's list of the 12 Apostles is a nickname Jesus gave John and his brother James. The name is *Boanerges*, which means, "Sons of Thunder." The brothers, hot-tempered and ambitious, lived up to the title.

One afternoon the disciples were arguing among themselves over which of them was the greatest. And John just had to get the last word in.

"Master," said John [apparently eager to establish his greatness], "we saw a man driving out demons in Your name and we tried to stop him because he was not one of us."

But Jesus corrected John: "Do not stop him," Jesus said, "for whoever is not against you is for you" (Luke 9:49-50).

Sons of Thunder.

Immediately following this incident, a controversy arose over the cold reception Jesus received at a certain Samaritan village. James and John were ready to warm things up. "Lord, do you want us to call fire down from heaven to destroy them?" (Luke 9:54) Jesus turned and rebuked the two brothers.

Sons of Thunder.

Another time, James and John approached Jesus with what seemed to them a logical request: "Teacher," they said, "we want You to do for us whatever we ask."

"What do you want Me to do for you?" He asked.

They replied, "Let one of us sit at Your right and the other at Your left in Your glory" (Mark 10:35-37).

Jesus explained that they didn't know what they were asking and that He would not be passing out the seats anyway; His Father would. What follows is Jesus' eloquent description of leadership: "Whoever wants to become great among you must be your servant" (Mark 10:43).

Sons of Thunder.

Sixty years later, as John wrote his letter, he could reflect on those years trudging with Jesus through the countryside of Palestine. And this much was indisputable: God had made John's life better. His wreckless zeal had been replaced by love. He wasn't any less enthusiastic, but the enthusiasm was directed now, controlled. Jesus Christ, whom he had seen, heard, and touched, had changed John. The Son of Thunder had become a Son of Love.

"We proclaim to you," John said, "what we have seen and heard, so that you also may have fellowship with us. And our fellowship is with the Father and

> *Jesus' friend John used to be called a son of Thunder. But Jesus was able to change him into a Son of Love. What about me?*
> *People call me a lot of things,*
> *but Son of Love isn't one of them.*

with His Son, Jesus Christ. We write this to make our joy complete" (1 John 1:3-4).

Complete Joy

With his life so significantly changed, John's joy is understandable. But that joy went beyond his own changed life. The source of John's joy was the One who made the changes—Jesus Christ. John's life and his letter focus not on himself but on Jesus. That focus on Jesus is clear in 1 John 1:1-4, where the following pattern emerges:

PREEXISTENCE *Jesus is God. He has always existed.*

"From the beginning" (1:1)—moving throughout the ages, without beginning, without end, Jesus Christ has existed. It didn't start in the manger. "With the Father" (1:2)—Jesus is on an equal level with God. John expresses the same thought in his Gospel: "In the beginning was the Word, and the Word was with God, and the Word was God" (John 1:1).

INCARNATION *Jesus became a man. He became flesh and blood.*

"We have heard... seen... touched" (1 John 1:1). "Appeared... seen it ... appeared" (1:2). "Seen... heard" (1:3). Jesus joined the human race. His body was real. John could hear Him, see Him, touch Him. As John expressed it in his Gospel: "The Word became flesh and lived for a while among us. We have seen His glory, the glory of the one and only Son, who came from the Father, full of grace and truth" (John 1:14).

PROCLAMATION *John shared the Good News.*

"This we proclaim" (1 John 1:1). "We

Son of Thunder, Son of Love / 21

FELLOWSHIP

testify to it ... we proclaim to you" (1:2). "We proclaim" (1:3). Once we meet Him and realize who He is, we want to introduce others to Him.

The result: We share together in eternal life.

"So that you also may have fellowship with us. And our fellowship is with the Father and with His Son, Jesus Christ" (1:3). Through faith we share together in eternal life, God's life. And so John speaks of complete joy (1:4).

The pattern should be no different today. Discovery should prompt sharing.

Here's Your Change

There's something about the ocean that brings out almost every conceivable emotion—from thunderous exuberance to brooding moodiness. I leaned against a weather-worn lifeguard tower at Manhattan Beach, California as the late afternoon was giving way to early evening. Occasionally the setting sun would force its way through the charcoal-gray overcast sky. And each time the clouds parted and the sun appeared, a shimmering silver ribbon of light danced across the surf. I sat down in the cold sand, absorbing the emotion of the moment, and retraced in my mind the past six months of my new life.

I recalled a Tuesday evening in January, standing in the church parking lot with my pastor friend. We had talked about other things, but the main thing I remembered was his simple challenge: "One person, who really believed God, could turn this city upside down!"

I thought about a series of weekly workshops I had attended on sharing Christianity with friends. On the first night, the workshop leader had asked, "Who here could lead someone to Christ using nothing but a Bible?" I had immediately flashed my hand into the air. No way was I going to be the only one of the 80 kids with his hand down. But only 5 of us had raised our hands, and we were called to the front to demonstrate. Problem was, I couldn't do it. I learned in a hurry.

Then came the weekly, door-to-door visits in the neighborhood surrounding the church. Six of us in the youth group were going to do it: We were going to turn the city upside down. How many doors had been slammed in my face over the past months? Screen doors, wooden doors ... even louvered windows!

During the last couple months of my senior year, fellow students at my high school had detected the change in my life. Most of them didn't understand.

Then the day after high school graduation, I left to spend three weeks at Manhattan Beach, sharing Christianity with children, youth, and adults. The changes in me over the past six months had been incredible. And yet, as I sat on the damp sand, watching the pounding Pacific breakers and the sun flashing through angry storm clouds, I was not nearly so impressed by the changes in my life as I was by the Person who was changing me.

Believing and obeying God, I concluded, is no great

credit to the person who believes or obeys. The credit goes to the One whom John heard, saw, touched, proclaimed—Jesus Christ.

The discovery just has to be shared: God can make life better!

What happens when this new discovery seems to complicate life? When you're suddenly very aware that you just don't measure up?

TWO

GOD IS LIGHT, WALK IN LIGHT

1 John 1:5–2:2

I wouldn't have dared to *say* it; that would have seemed an insult to God. After all, when someone does so much for you, it's not nice to quibble over the details.

Even so, I had a disturbing thought rattling around in my brain. God can make life better, and in many ways He had improved mine. But there were times as a new Christian that life did not *seem* better. In fact, it seemed worse. And that's what I would not have dared to say at the time. But it was true. In at least one way, things had become more complicated since I had become a Christian.

I had gone to church camps and retreats and seminars and special meetings. I had made resolution after resolution: *My life is going to be different*! But like the yearbook photographs I posed for every fall, things didn't always turn out as I hoped. My efforts to change seemed useless.

Was life really better?

John said, "This is the message we have heard from Him and declare to you: God is light; in Him there is no darkness at all" (1 John 1:5).

But after becoming a Christian, there were times when I felt far more dark than before. Dirty and unfit.

Arrows Don't Earn Points

Ever notice how easy it is to take directions for granted? For example, when was the last time you felt warm, grateful feelings for a stop sign? Or when did you last say a silent thank-you for a grocery store sign telling you: "Express Lane—10 items or less"? Honestly, do one-way arrows on street corners give you chills of excitement?

Good directions are underappreciated and often disregarded. And when you choose to ignore the good directions—the stop sign, express-lane sign, one-way sign—seeing the message can be embarrassing, irritating.

You notice the stop sign, but decide to slip by without making a full stop. But a cop pulls you over and points to the bright red, octagonal sign as he slips a tablet out of his pocket.

You have 15 items in your shopping cart, not 10. But you're in a hurry, and besides, will the clerk really care anyway? But the large lady behind you clears her throat and says loudly to her friend, "Oh, look Mabel, the sign says 10 items or less! Doesn't it irk you when people try to sneak through with more?"

You didn't plan to defy the one-way traffic. Now that

God Is Light, Walk in Light / 27

you have, the last thing you want staring you in the face is a sign to remind you of your blunder. You feel foolish enough and you're already looking for a way to turn around . . . *fast*.

Directional arrows don't earn points. We either follow them, while taking them for granted, or we ignore them and try to forget them. But what is Christianity? In a sense, it's a system of directional arrows, pointing us to a new way of living. In time we may learn to take the arrows to heart, joyfully following their direction. But often, especially as new Christians, those directional arrows are annoying reminders of changes that need to be made. God can make life better. But it's often a painful process.

Like a directional arrow in my spirit, Christianity made me aware of sin. It pointed out my wrong thoughts, actions, habits. And it showed me the way to get rid of the guilt. I had accepted Jesus' offer of complete forgiveness, paid for by His death, guaranteed by His resurrection.

After I became a Christian though, that awareness of sin did not evaporate. The directional arrows were still there. And that made God seem distant, and me, unworthy. The thing that had brought me close, now seemed to separate me.

The question came: "OK, now how do I handle these guilt feelings?"

State Your Claim

That question demands an answer. To become a Christian and yet be so aware of your shortcomings breeds internal conflict. You have to find a way to resolve the hassle.

Some people merely jettison their faith. *If I don't claim to be a Christian, maybe I won't feel so bad when I live like a garbage can.* Other people cheapen their definition of morality. They redefine sin. *If I don't call it sin, maybe I won't feel so immoral.* Still others find a peculiar, hard-to-explain joy in guilt: It points them to forgiveness. They don't like feeling guilty, but they appreciate feeling clean when they've made things right. If I don't notice my wrong, how will it ever be made right? In 1 John 1:5—2:2, John looks at sin and presents:

3 claims,
3 consequences, and
3 better ideas.

The background to these three "3s" is John's simple statement: "God is light; in Him there is no darkness at all" (1:5).

With that in mind, consider *claim #1:* "If we claim to have fellowship with Him yet walk in the darkness, we lie and do not live by the truth" (1:6).

We can look into the light, God's moral perfection, and claim that we have fellowship with Him. We share things in common with Him. We can *say* we are genuine, sincere, honest, real, changed-life Christians ... so changed that we are like God Himself. We have fellowship with God. We are on common moral ground with the Creator.

"Yet walk in darkness" (1:6).

Consequence #1: "We lie and do not live by the truth" (1:6).

Truth is not just something you *say*, it's something

God Is Light, Walk in Light / 29

you *do*, something you *live*. Our lives have to match our claims. We cannot unload our moral grime as long as we insist we don't have any to unload. *Saying* we share God's holiness does not make it happen; there has to be a change. And that's....

Better idea #1: "But if we walk in the light, as He is in the light, we have fellowship with one another, and the blood of Jesus, His Son, purifies us from every sin" (1:7).

If I claim I have fellowship with the One who is light, I have to walk in the light. I must be moral, new, different, changed. Problem: Based on my experience, that kind of total-light change is not fully attainable. That is precisely my problem—a problem shared by others. I feel guilty for the darkness in my life. How can I brighten it up? I'm aware of my moral trash. How can I bag it and toss it out?

John answers these questions in a hurry, but first he clarifies, in case we can't wait, that he is not talking *perfection*. Well, he is, but he isn't. If you sin, God does not expect you to turn in your badge as a Christian. "The blood of Jesus, His Son, purifies us from every sin" (1:7).

Moral newness, living and walking in light, does not mean you are the same as God. It does demand that you see sin in a new light.

Halo? What Halo?

Claim #2: "If we claim to be without sin, we deceive ourselves and the truth is not in us" (1:8).

I've only had the experience once or twice, and it's

hard to keep a straight face. What *do* you say to a person who tells you, in all seriousness, that he never, ever sins.

I talked once with a scruffy, wild-eyed guy on a street corner in Hollywood. And this person had convinced himself that he'd arrived. In his mind, the runway had been cleared and he had landed and deplaned, but his immoral streak had been checked through to some other planet.

I suppose you needn't be particularly weird to come to the same conclusion. If you were to redefine sin, to lower the standards, or to ignore your conscience, you might persuade yourself you were sinless. Maybe.

But sin does not go away merely by ignoring it, or renaming it. We might say, for example, that lust is not really so bad, it's merely having normal human feelings. Stealing is getting what I figure I need from an available source. Pride is healthy self-confidence. Gossip is discussion.

In contrast, the Bible says, "The heart is deceitful above all things and beyond cure. Who can understand it?" (Jeremiah 17:9)

And that brings us to *consequence #2:* self-deception. "We deceive ourselves and the truth is not in us" (1 John 1:8).

What is *better idea #2?* "If we confess our sins, He is faithful and just and will forgive us our sins and purify us from all unrighteousness" (1:9).

"Confess" means agree—to say the same thing God says. God calls lust sin; I call *my* lust sin. God says pride is wrong; I say *my* pride is wrong. God thinks gossip is ugly; I agree that *my* gossip is ugly.

Nor does God give us the option of agreeing with

Him about *what sin is*, without agreeing with Him about *what to do with it*. You can't call lust sin and then wallow in it. You can't say pride is wrong and then spoon-feed your bloated ego. You can't agree that gossip is ugly and then spread those juicy stories to the world, person by interested person. Agreeing with God demands change. And how is the change achieved?

One writer describes this process as "living life with the roof off," in openness to God. I don't try to hide from Him, or blame my faults on society, my mother or dad, or my temperamental dog. I own up to my moral flubs and frustrating habits. I am open with God about each grungy detail. I share with Him my powerlessness, and I ask for His help.

His guaranteed response: *forgiveness, purification*!

It's Just That Simple, Huh?

But the question arises: how can God be considered *just* to forgive sin? If we've gotten used to the idea of forgiveness, we may be missing the impact.

Imagine a vicious dictator, ruthlessly taking life, slaughtering innocent people. Think of a Nero, a Hitler, an Idi Amin. One Christian watches as another is bashed to death in the Roman arena. A Jewish family looks on as a father or brother, sister or mother is hauled off to a concentration camp to endure abuse and death. An African is forced to watch as his friend is bludgeoned to death.

If you had the power to see that justice was done, and chose instead to overlook cruelty, what would people think? If you ignored Nero's inhumanity, or

Hitler's, or Amin's, would people call you good, just, righteous? Or would they consider you spineless and unjust? A sense of justice demands that gross wrongs be punished.

But John insists that when God forgives, He is *good*. He is *faithful* when he forgives. He is *just*, *righteous*.

How can God be good and still forgive? How can He be considered faithful if He overlooks wrong? How can He remain just if He justifies people who sin? How can He be righteous, if He ignores unrighteousness?

The Apostle Paul answered that question in his letter to the church at Rome. "All have sinned," Paul said, "and fall short of the glory of God" (Romans 3:23). That includes not just the extra-foul dictators—but *all of us*. And, Paul goes on, we may all be "justified freely by His grace through the redemption that came by Christ Jesus" (v. 24). God accomplished all this, according to Paul, by sending His innocent Son to die for us. God "did this to demonstrate His justice . . . so as to be just and the One who justifies [declares righteous] the man who has faith in Jesus" (vv. 25-26).

God is *just*.

God is the *justifier*.

Both.

Simultaneously.

When we agree with God about our sin, when we own up to it, confess it, God freely forgives us because of the sacrifice of His Son. "He is faithful and just" to do so, John says (1 John 1:9).

But He doesn't regard sin lightly. He couldn't overlook immorality. And He didn't. God sacrificed His own Son so we wouldn't have to receive the punishment we really deserve. Forgiveness comes to us free, in a very *costly* way.

So how can we casually say, "Um, oh yeh, God, sorry 'bout that sin. Thanks for forgiving me, overlooking my wrong and everything."

We can say it. But we can never say it lightly.

Nope, Can't Say as I Have. . . .

It's one thing to claim we never sin. It's another thing to say, "I *never have* sinned." It's almost easier to side with the guy who says he never sins. We *might* figure he used to sin, but outgrew the habit. But to state *claim #3*, that we *never have* sinned, that's another story: "If we claim we have not sinned, we make Him out to be a liar, and His Word has no place in our lives" (1 John 1:10).

Consequence #3 involves that little word "liar." God says we have sinned. We cannot say otherwise without making God into a liar. Nor can we hang onto the parts of the Bible we like, say, "God is love" (1 John 4:8), and toss out the parts we find disagreeable, such as, "There is no one righteous, not even one" (Romans 3:10). If I say (*claim #3*), "I have not sinned," I (*consequence #3*) make God out to be a liar, and His Word (which calls me a sinner) has no place in my life.

Remember the backdrop, the setting for all these *claims, consequences, and better ideas:* "God is light; in Him there is no darkness at all" (1 John 1:5). He expects there to be changes in us. We are to "walk in the light as He is in the light" (1:7). Or as Peter put it, "Just as He who called you is holy, so be holy in all you do; for it is written: 'Be holy, because I am holy' "

(1 Peter 1:15). We must have a realistic image of ourselves. We must be able to recognize our moral crud when we see it. And having seen it, we must own up to it.

The solution to *claim #3* and *consequence #3* is God's *better idea #3:* "My dear children, I write this to you so that you will not sin. But if anybody does sin, we have one who speaks to the Father in our defense—Jesus Christ, the Righteous One. He is the atoning sacrifice for our sins, and not only for ours, but also for the sins of the whole world" (1 John 2:1-2).

John talks about people who claim to have a special relationship with God and yet sin; and he talks about people who claim they never sin; and he talks about people who claim they never did sin . . . not even once. And he stacks all that up and concludes: You can't claim to have special favors with God and then live a garbage-can life. But neither can you say, "Sin? Me? Course not!"

"Walking in the light" does not mean sinlessness. John sketches a realistic portrait of us all. We are people who still fall short, and we have a voice inside us that knows it.

What should happen when that voice screams, "Guilty!"? We should be honest and open with God who knows all things (1 John 1:9). But we should not be afraid we'll be expelled from God's kingdom. He will forgive us and cleanse us if we turn to Him.

That, after all, is why He put that voice inside us. So that, when we do sin, we will be driven, not *away* from Him, but *to* Him. Then, weakness by weakness, God can begin to turn us into people of moral strength. Every time we win a contest against immorality, we will become stronger, more like God Himself, who is perfect light.

But when we sin, something also happens in heaven. Something beautifully peculiar. Jesus Christ Himself comes to our defense (1 John 2:1). It's not that God the Father and God the Son get into a scuffle over our wrongdoing—the Father against us, the Son for us. It's not even that there is a big debate about it, with the young attorney, Jesus, winning out. God, we might say, "agrees with Himself" that Jesus' sacrifice paid for our sin.

The point is, each moral slip is not only a reminder of our weakness; it is also a reminder of the strength of God's forgiveness. Why? Because Jesus, God Himself, became the sacrifice for our bent nature (2:2). There is no sin we can ever commit that can overpower the sacrifice of God Himself.

That's not our ticket to scuzzy living.

It's further proof that God can make life better.

I can't wallow in sin.
I can't say I'm sinless.
I run from evil, but good is
  out of reach.
Who am I then?
And how can I ever be sure
I am truly Christian?

THREE

OLD COMMANDMENT, NEW COMMANDMENT

1 John 2:3-11

It's a standard restaurant antic:

You just pour out a few grains of salt—a teaspoon or less will do. Then, carefully, you balance the salt shaker at an angle. If you do it just so, you can create your own iodized leaning tower. The grains of salt provide just enough friction to keep the glass container from falling.

Congratulations! You've just achieved balance.

Tediously.

Unnecessarily.

Salt shakers, after all, are provided with nice, stable, flat bases on which to rest.

As Christians we are the salt of the earth, provided with a way to balanced, stable living. Our spiritual security does not have to be a constant question. We don't have to fear falling. If we carelessly mess around with our balance, we may fall. But it just doesn't have

38 / New and Improved

to be that way at all.

So why do we sometimes wonder if we can ever be right with God? And how *can* we be sure our Christian lives are stable?

Not Hope, Not Think, No Way!

How well I recall the early days of my "Christian experience," and the concern more mature Christians expressed. They wanted to make sure I could deal with my doubts.

Their answer: an interesting phenomenon called "assurance of salvation." After all, why should anyone waste his whole life with needless questions about his relationship with God?

In all honesty, I had good reason to question my relationship with God. Asking myself the question, "Is God mad at me?" wasn't all bad. Jesus had harsh words for hypocrites (Matthew 23). And at the time, I was living an amazingly hypocritical lifestyle: active in the church, sinning like crazy everywhere else.

What did I need to hear?

The people who saw me at church (though at times I'm sure *they* wondered) offered me "assurance of salvation." This "assurance" took the form of 1 John 5:13: "I write these things to you who believe in the name of the Son of God so that you may know that you have eternal life." To which the church people added: "Not think, not hope, but *know.*"

OK, no doubts now.

Problem: *In my condition, was it true that I had no need to worry, no need to wonder?*

Old Commandment, New Commandment / 39

Years later, my life beautifully, though not yet completely, rearranged, I began sharing Christianity with others. I'd tell them how to become Christians, say a few words about prayer or Bible reading, or church attendance, and then add my pitch on "assurance of salvation." I wanted to head off their doubts, anticipate their questions, give 'em the verse: "Not think, not hope, but *know.*"

But my approach has shifted a bit since those days. After all, when John said, "these things," (1 John 5:13), what did he mean? He was thinking of the contents of the letter he was writing—1 John.

"Walk in the light" (1:7).
"Confess sin" (1:9).
"Obey His commands" (2:3).
"Do not love the world" (2:15).
"Love one another" (3:11).
Etc.

Can we ignore the *these things* of 1 John, and then tell ourselves, "Not think, not hope, but *know*"? Can we feel stable, secure, if we insist on living like a garbage heap? Or is that trying to balance the salt shaker on edge—maybe we'll stand, maybe we'll fall?

Love Laws

I suspect people came to the Apostle John with the question, "How can I be sure I'm a Christian?" Maybe they told him of their efforts to live right and their tendency to live wrong. Maybe they said, "I followed Jesus for a while, then turned away. Am I still a Christian? Or has God drummed me out of His family?"

40 / New and Improved

Commands that are hard to follow:

- Love your neighbor as yourself.
- Don't worry about tomorrow.
- Give thanks in everything.
- Don't let the sun go down on your anger.
- Don't be jealous.
- Watch your tongue.
- Don't judge other people.

(All of the above!)

Old Commandment, New Commandment / 41

This letter, 1 John, is his answer. And 1 John 2:3-11 tackles two related questions. *Question #1: How can I know that I know God?* We can be sure we know Him, "if we obey His commands" (v. 3).

File this key word in your mind: *commands*.

Initially, what I liked about Christianity was the ease of it. God lifted my guilt, welcomed me into His family, poured out His favors. He was good. Christianity was easy. That key word, *commands*, was something I hadn't reckoned with. And since it's so much fun to talk about the love of God, it's easy to gloss over His royal expectations, His commands.

There used to be a popular saying, "Trust God and do whatever you want." Maybe some Christians still spout it. It sounds attractive. We all want to do *whatever we want*. The quote's camouflaged catch is: *If you truly trust God, you'll want to do His will.* Clever. There's truth in the saying. But it skirts the unpleasant word: *commands.*

For me the problem was, every time I turned a page in my black leather Bible, God was giving another command, outlining another expectation, laying before me a lifestyle. Commands, commands, commands.

And why so many? Because we can't live without them. If I construct my life without them, I build a mess, a living disaster. Many Christians know that, and learn to welcome His commands. But the person who constantly ignores God's clear commands is raising a question mark as to whether he really knows God.

"The man who says, 'I trust Him,' but does not do what He commands is a liar, and the truth is not in him" (v. 4).

On the other hand: "If anyone obeys His Word, God's

love is truly made complete in him" (v. 5).

God's love and His commands go together. The commands are God's love laws.

Love Walk

This section of 1 John (2:3-11) tackles a second question—*question #2: How can I know that my life is linked up with God's?*

"This is how we know that we are in Him: Whoever claims to live in Him must walk as Jesus did" (2:5-6).

God's commands give the outline of the picture. To fill in the empty places, look at Jesus. So, here's another key word to lock away next to commands: *walk*.

I enjoy John's phrase, "Walk as Jesus did." Apparently John liked the concept too. In the first chapter of his letter he pictures Jesus' life as a walk. And after mentioning it here, he doesn't drop it altogether; he will pick it up again. This idea of Jesus' walk—take a look.

Picture: During the festivities of a wedding in Cana of Galilee, the beverage supply runs low. Concern for the young bride and groom motivates Jesus to transform H_2O into vintage wine. As Jesus walks through the story you pick up some insight into His sensitivity to the needs of people (John 2:1-11).

Walk as He walked: *Live in concerned sensitivity.*

Picture: Jesus steps into the temple, God's house. The religious leaders have turned the place into a carnival, selling sacrifices and ripping off worshipers to line the pockets of their tunics. In anger, Jesus empties the place (John 2:12-25).

Walk as He walked: *Hate sin*.

Picture: A religious leader has questions. As a religious leader—a teacher—he should already know the answers. But his questions are honest, and Jesus stays up late explaining the basic principles of the kingdom of God. The Father's love for the world was so intense, Jesus explains, that He freely gave the gift of His Son. Anyone who believed would not come to destruction, but would inherit the gift of eternal life. The Father loved. The Son loved. God gave (John 3:1-21).

Walk as He walked: *Practice self-sacrificing love*.

The pictures go on throughout John's Gospel, one impression after another. Impressions of love, of concern for people, of selflessness. Taken together, the Gospel of John forms a mural of the life of Christ, a panorama of how *we* should live. At the conclusion of his Gospel, John is overwhelmed with the image, God walking among us in the Person of Jesus. And he says, "Jesus did many other things as well. If every one of them were written down, I suppose that even the whole world would not have room for the books that would be written" (John 21:25).

If John's Gospel is not that comprehensive, cosmic library, what is it? It is one comparatively small collection of word pictures, portraying how Christ walked. "Whoever claims to live in Him must walk as Jesus did" (1 John 2:6).

Command Performance

Reach into your mind and retrieve that first key word: *Command*.

It will give you a handle on where John is headed next. He is about to come at the word *command* from a different angle:

"Dear friends, I am not writing you a new command but an old one, which you have had since the beginning. This old command is the message you have heard. Yet I am writing you a new command; its truth is seen in Him and you, because the darkness is passing and the true light is already shining" (1 John 2:7-8).

What's the point? Is John talking about one command, or two? New or old? And the answer is yes, yes, both, both.

The command is not something entirely new and different. It is basic. It has roots in what it means to be Christian.

The "old" command is the message we've heard: God is holy light. We are dirty dark. Through the Father's Son we are made clean and new. We have fellowship with God. We walk in the light (1 John 1). The command is old.

But the command is also "new." "Its truth," John says, "is seen in Him and you" (2:8).

Huh? Like an old fruit tree that blossoms new each year, there is a continual newness to the old command. It is fulfilled and re-fulfilled with each new person who joins God's family.

Moreover, within John's lifetime, God has done something entirely new, something that had not happened in all of history: God became a man. Christ walked on our planet. The old command was given new texture, new meaning.

What old command?

And what *new* command?

Specifically Now . . .

Imagine someone you know who has become a Christian. Pick someone whose life, you feel, has been solidly changed. What's different? How are they new? How is life better for them?

As I've thought about those questions, conjured my own impressions, over and over again my mind reaches for the same word: *love*. I can think of people who used to be gruff and now are mellow. I can think of people who used to steal, and now give. I can think of people who were recklessly ambitious, but now have room in their peripheral vision for someone else. Think of whomever you want—liars who are truthful; "lust-ers" who are pure; average, good people with a new side to their "average goodness"—*love* is there somewhere.

Christianity—true Christianity—will not sit on the shelf next to hate; it will shove it off. Quietly, love will destroy anything that stands in it's way. Love is the old/new commandment.

Reach back into your memory for the second word: *walk*. And watch John weave it all together—command, walk, love.

"Anyone who claims to be in the light but hates his brother is still in the darkness. Whoever loves his brother lives in the light, and there is nothing in him to make him stumble. But whoever hates his brother is in the darkness and walks around in the darkness; he does not know where he is going, because the darkness has blinded him" (1 John 2:9-11).

I read all these verses (1 John 2:3-11), and I say, "John, pull some order out of these random thoughts!"

Then I reread them, and remember:

"Hearing that Jesus had silenced the Sadducees, the Pharisees got together. One of them, an expert in the Law, tested Him with this question: 'Teacher, which is the greatest commandment in the Law?'

"Jesus replied: 'Love the Lord your God with all your heart, with all your soul, and with all your mind.' This is the first and greatest commandment. And the second is like it: 'Love your neighbor as yourself.' All the Law and the Prophets hang on these two commandments" (Matthew 22:34-40).

The commands of God all hang on love: love for God. But Jesus refused to separate love for God from love for others. Wonder why?

Loving God, knowing God, is tied to loving others. You may be able to love your neighbor and not love God. But you *cannot* love God and hate your neighbor. Repeat: You cannot love God and hate your neighbor. God's love will not sit on the shelf next to hate. It'll shove it off. *Crash!* New life! *Better* life!

So I'm not sinless, but I do love God. How do I measure my love for God? I've tried various approaches: If I pitch my tent in the church building, make it my home away from home, I love God. If I put my Bible on a stand covering the TV screen, I love God. If I quit talking to people and pray all the time instead, I love God. If I feel super, physically and emotionally, if a warm glow settles over me, I love God. Really?

The problem is, none of those measurements line up with the Bible's standard. Instead, John says if you want to check the health of your love for God, check your love for other people. Loving God is hard to measure. Loving people is out in the open, clear for inspection.

I may stumble and fall. I may flirt with the idea of balancing my life on edge—trying to be upright and loose at the same time. But if I begin to wonder about God's love for me and my love for God, I won't carelessly quote 1 John 5:13 with the verbal caboose; "Not think, not hope, but *know.*" Instead, I'll go back to the basics. I'll check the old/new commandment: Am I walking as Jesus walked? In love?

Sometimes I ask myself:
Why am I sure I know God?
Why is it enough to be forgiven?
What does my Christianity mean to me now?

FOUR

NEW LIFE, NEW PERIL
1 John 2:12-17

When it comes to plants, I am a first-class klutz. You name it, I can put it out of its misery. Swedish ivy? Spider plants? Madagascar palm? A day or two under my watchful eye and there will be nothing left but a pot of dirt and a withered shoot.

I have noticed that certain plants yield to destruction more readily than others. Generally, plants are most susceptible when they're most delicate—delicate because they are young and because it's their nature to be delicate.

Whoa! I feel an object lesson coming on. ...

Remember Jesus' story about different kinds of soil, different growing conditions? (Matthew 13:1-23) The farmer follows the agricultural approach of his day: he scatters seed. Rather than making tidy little holes, plunking down the seed, and covering it, the farmer grabs a handful of seeds and pitches it across the field.

In the process . . . some lands on the path. It's bound to happen. Toss seed around like that, and you never can tell where it will spring up. Or not spring up. And once devoured by fowl friends, there will be no growth.

Some seeds hit the dirt, but it's rocky dirt. No room for root. Plants sprout up, but not down. The blistering sun shines down—*sizzle*!—it's all over. Withered plants are dead plants.

Some seeds hit the dirt, but weeds are all around. The seeds are surrounded. Thorns to the left of them. Weeds to the right of them. Thistles before them. Tares behind them. No way are those weedy seeds going to make it. The thorns will choke the life out of them.

But some seeds make their way into good soil. When they do, watch out! They grow! Some seeds produce 100 percent, some 60, some 30.

Problem: The instant the seeds are scattered, it's hard to tell which ones will make it and which ones will dud out. Even after a green sprout pushes its way into the light of day, its destiny still appears to be up for grabs. You've got to wait around. Fruitfulness will make the point. Or barrenness.

Some "potential Christians" have footpath ears. Some have cobblestone hearts. Others have thorn-infested minds. But some are good, receptive ground. Faith roots deep in them.

Christianity seems to be a lot like my office greenhouse. Everything is against the survival of the plants. I don't generally stuff stones in the soil, put plants under heat lamps, or try to graft in a little crabgrass. Even so, I manage to produce adequate peril to endanger any species.

Now, according to the laws of nature, seeds and

plants that are treated right should grow. But every time a Christian makes it, it's not natural, it's supernatural. Christians are in a hostile environment. And Satan's birds are after them.

That's why Christians should worry if they are not growing. And that's why there's a lot of rejoicing when they are growing.

Of Plants and People

Plants grow like Christians grow. Some plants are tender new shoots—full of the joy of new life. Some are stable, stately trees—rooted and settled. Others are vibrant, fast-growing plants—overcoming the elements. And there are Christians to match—*children, fathers, young men*. John interrupts the progress of his thoughts twice to comment on these three stages of Christian growth.

First word to children: "I write to you, dear children, because your sins have been forgiven on account of His name" (1 John 2:12).

It all starts here. Forgiveness brings life, and with it, the basis and hope of growth.

First word to fathers: "I write to you, fathers, because you have known Him who is from the beginning" (v. 13).

Some people know God, and other people *know* God. These mature Christians John mentions, on the far end of growth, *know* God. They may know the Bible. They may know theology. But beyond the religious things they know about, they know God. Personally. One-to-one. Let that simmer—or to follow the plant analogy, let it soak in.

First word to young men: "I write to you, young men, because you have overcome the evil one" (v. 13).

Remember? Christians are planted in a hostile environment. Growth is supernatural. But with God's help it happens. You can overcome rather than be overcome. Bad influences don't have to wither your spiritual leaves. Evil elements needn't tangle your roots.

Second word to children: "I write to you, dear children, because you have known the Father" (v. 13).

God's forgiveness makes us part of His family; that's what plants the seed (v. 12). What happens? We know God. But *how* do we know Him? How do we relate to Him? What do we call Him? Father! And when we come to see who He is, quite naturally, we obey Him as obedient sons.

Second word to fathers: "I write to you, fathers, because you have known Him who is from the beginning" (v. 14).

Sound familiar? With some difficulty, I will resist the temptation to repeat my comment about John's comment. Once you've said the plant is mature, sturdy, vibrant, green, rooted, what more should be said? The plant is mature, sturdy, vibrant, green, rooted. Repeat reading for added emphasis.

Second word to young men: "I write to you, young men, because you are strong, and the Word of God lives in you, and you have overcome the evil one" (v. 14).

This verse is likewise familiar. But this time it has an added emphasis. *How* do strong spiritual young men overcome? Through God's Word—God's living Word. "The Word of God is living and active. Sharper than any double-edged sword, it penetrates even to dividing soul and spirit, joints and marrow; it judges the thoughts and attitudes of the heart" (Hebrews 4:12).

Interestingly, the writer of Hebrews goes on to say, "Nothing in all creation is hidden from God's sight. Everything is uncovered and laid bare before the eyes of Him to whom we must give account" (v. 13).

We don't doubt that God sees things as they really are. But Hebrews links God's perception of us—the way *He* sees us—with the way we can see ourselves. We can see ourselves *as God sees us.* How? Through His living and active Word. Is it surprising, then, that spiritually strong young men can overcome "the evil one"? They have an incredible resource, the ultimate plant food.

Root Inspection

Imagine Jeff: He comes from an average home. But his folks are not particularly sympathetic to his new "religious discovery." He's a gung-ho Christian. They are as disinterested in his faith as a dog offered Gravy Train when he's already chomping a T-bone steak. (The "steak" they claim is hassle-free, successful living.) Why add God to their busy schedule?

Let's say, further, that Jeff has had his share of bad habits to break. Every day, or so it seems, he is finding a new area of his life that God wants to control. He just knows he has to be "more committed."

To complete the picture, let's assume that Jeff has a few friends who are concerned about his spiritual welfare. They don't quite have their own foliage transplanted into godly soil, but they are nonetheless eager to inspect Jeff's Gospel roots. They tell him how he ought to be praying, where he should go, what he should do, where he shouldn't go, what he shouldn't do. They want to monitor his Bible study, tell him who to date, and guide him to the proper pew in church.

Before long, Jeff is getting uptight. He's trying to spiritually second-guess his Christian friends, and he's developing paranoia and guilt feelings over everything. Does he own a Christian tape deck? Is his haircut devout? Does he brush his teeth like a man of God?

Then one day Jeff cracks open his New Testament and tumbles into 1 John. Remember, John sets an incredibly high standard; he does not offer cheap "assurance of salvation." John calls for a changed life to back up our claim to be Christian. John agrees with Jesus: "Not everyone who says to Me, 'Lord, Lord,' will enter the kingdom of heaven, but only he who does the will of My Father who is in heaven" (Matthew 7:21).

So, reading 1 John could easily send Jeff sliding further into the pits. With the meddling of his well-meaning friends, and the strong message of 1 John, Jeff could sink in guilt and cash in his Christianity.

Except . . . 1 John anticipated that problem. As John sat down to write his letter, he included strong words of encouragement alongside strong words of caution—words to "dear children," words to spiritual "fathers," words to overcoming "young men."

In this balance of assurance and warning, it's as if John wants us to walk a thin line. We are not to be overcome with doubt concerning our relationship with God. But neither are we to feel confident if our style of life does not measure up.

God can make life better. But if ours isn't, we'd better check our roots.

Where Love Should Land

An exercise in fantasy:

Tomorrow you face a mammoth test. It will determine a third of your final grade. You get home by 3:45 and immediately hit the books. Concerned over the probable outcome of the test, you study through the dinner hour, a bowl of chips and Pepsi at your side. You study into the evening hours.

At 11:30 your head bobs. You realize you have read and reread the same line three times. More Pepsi. A candy bar. And onward. By 3 A.M. you're wasted, but you figure as close as it is to dawn, and as precarious your grade, you'll make it an all-nighter. To make that happen, you need some fresh air. *A walk through the nearby park will do,* you tell yourself.

As you step out the door, a blast of cool night air takes your breath away. Instantly, you are revived. In perfect quiet you walk the two blocks to the park. Crossing the street, you notice just how still, how peaceful, how dark nighttime can be.

The sidewalk snakes through the park, around bushes and trees, past a fountain. It stretches straight across an open field, then past another wooded area. But here the shadows, cast by moonlight filtering through tree branches, play tricks on you. You suddenly feel creepy.

You're sure you are being watched, but you chase such juvenile suspicions out of your mind.

Then you hear it. It's undeniable. You whirl around, but not fast enough. You are knocked backward by the sheer weight of it. It had been so silent; its leap so effortless. You are flat on your back now, peering into the savage face of. . . .

Surprise. It's the element of the unexpected that gets us. It's the unforeseen that defeats us.

"Be self-controlled and alert. Your enemy the devil prowls around like a roaring lion looking for someone to devour" (1 Peter 5:8).

The devil often overtakes us unexpectedly. And his favorite thicket to hide behind is our ignorance of his approach, our clouded understanding of his style.

But in addition to the devil, we have an equally dangerous enemy that also escapes our notice. Strangely enough, this enemy has to do with "love."

Love Divided

"Love," someone said, "is multiplied as it is given away." But we might insert, "love cannot be divided."

"Do not love the world," John said, "or anything in the world" (1 John 2:15).

Now there is the world, and there is the *world*. For instance, God says He loves the world (John 3:16), and He means the human race. He created the world (John 1:10), and was pleased with the result (Genesis 1:31). But there is a "world order" that He is not fond of at all. This world is in the grip of the evil one (1 John 5:19).

As Paul put it, "You were dead in your transgressions and sins, in which you used to live when you followed the ways of this world and of the ruler of the kingdom of the air, the spirit who is now at work in those who are disobedient" (Ephesians 2:1-2).

The point is, there is an old way of living, an outlook on life that even as Christians we are easily entangled in. And when our roots begin to sink into this world's soil, we begin to die. It happens slowly, and we hardly notice it at first. That's why we have to be warned of the peril. Without the warning, we might make ourselves at home with the world and begin to wither without even knowing it.

So the Apostle James says, "Don't you know that friendship with the world is hatred toward God? Anyone who chooses to be a friend of the world becomes an enemy of God" (James 4:4).

Who would choose to be God's enemy for the sake of friendship with this world's system? Well, if we knew the difference, if we saw and understood, perhaps few of us would. But if God seems remote, and the world seems real, and we figure we can have both, then perhaps. . . .

But John says we can't have both. And Jesus says the same. "No one can serve two masters. Either he will hate the one and love the other, or he will be devoted to the one and despise the other" (Matthew 6:24).

We careen toward destruction when we don't see that both God and the world are incredibly demanding. No matter how much we give either one of them, they expect more, until they have everything we can possibly give.

And the Problem is . . .

Once either God or the world gets hold of you, they will not let go. John makes this point three ways:

God/world conflict #1: No room for two. "If anyone loves the world, the love of the Father is not in him" (1 John 2:15).

Love of the world and love of God are mutually exclusive. Like opposite poles of a magnet, they repel each other. Like love and hate, they will not share the same shelf. One pushes the other off.

God/world conflict #2: Different origins. "For everything in the world—the cravings of sinful man, the lust of his eyes, and the boasting of what he has and does—comes not from the Father but from the world" (1 John 2:16).

God will teach us to harness our cravings. He will put our desires into proper perspective. He will teach us how to use our possessions. But when we fall in love with the world, listen uncritically to our cravings, feed our lusts, stroke our possessions, we've stopped listening to the Father. We've switched affections. We've stepped zombie-like to the edge of spiritual disaster.

God/world conflict #3: Not everything endures. "The world and its desires pass away, but the man who does the will of God lives forever" (1 John 2:17).

Strange isn't it, the way God turns things around? Right now, God seems so remote; the world so real. God seems by His absence, so puny and weak; the world by its commanding presence so strong, so permanent. All that will change! In an instant, this life, the world, will seem a faint and distant dream. The inescapable and awesome reality, by comparison the only reality, will be God.

God and ... God and those who do His will now.

God can make life better. Knowing Him is the beginning. Forgiveness is a basic starting point. But Christianity is so much more.

You want to be strong.
But with all the weird teachings
masquerading as Christianity,
how can you be sure
you know the truth?

FIVE
IN THE CHURCH, IN THE TRUTH
1 John 2:18-27

I suppose most Christians have certain fears about sharing their faith. I have mine. But one evening as a couple of us stood on Hollywood Boulevard talking to people about Christianity, the conversation was going surprisingly well. I don't mean that every passerby dropped at our feet, begging for the privilege of turning to Christ. Hardly. But we were enjoying a good reception. People were listening. We were establishing a relaxed rapport that bordered on friendship.

Then it happened.

A brightly painted bus came tooling down the boulevard, in the bumper-to-bumper traffic, windows down. And this busload of religious freaks was alive with the sound of music—top-of-their-lungs music.

The people we were talking to sort of looked at each other uneasily, clipped off a couple of remarks, and unleashed a few laughs. As we continued our con-

62 / New and Improved

versation I noticed the bus turn onto a side street at the end of the block.

A few minutes later, a bunch of scruffy religionists with guitars surrounded us. Next thing I knew, they were singing again. And it wasn't a serenade.

You better get right with God
Don't be a hypocrite
You better quit
Doin' your own thing
'Cause the Lord is tired of it!

Over and over they sang/chanted their ditty, drowning out our conversation about Christianity. I couldn't believe it. Our new acquaintances, not yet "part of the fold," were spooked and beat a hasty retreat, leaving us to face this band of musical prophets.

"What are you trying to accomplish?" I asked.

"You've got to drop out of the system," they told me. "If you don't forsake all, you're not worthy of Christ."

What followed was a lengthy discussion—perhaps debate is a more accurate word—about selling our possessions, dropping out of school, hating everything including our families, giving all our money to their group and joining them in a communal "family." All of this, they insisted, for the sake of Christ. If we didn't agree, we were worthy only of hell fire.

For the rest of the evening, every time we tried to talk to someone about Christ, we were again surrounded by this band of dissenters, singing their warning with voices at full throttle. Very discouraging.

That particular religious group later became one of the most outlandish and perverted cults to come out of "Christianity": "the Children of God," later renamed "the Family of Love."

Perhaps cults never start out as odd as they become. But many waste little time falling into full-tilt weirdness. It's not just that they are out of step with the rest of the world. We could all stand to be a bit odd in that sense. But they are often in conflict with what they claim to promote. They insist they are speaking for God and wind up speaking against Him. They say they want to further His plan, but obstruct it. In the process, a lot of sincere people become confused, misled.

And the Time Is . . .

The confusion is not new. Cultish "Christianity" is not new. As long as Christianity has been around, anti-Christians have been muddying up the spiritual waters. And thirsty Christians have been wondering if it's OK to swallow it.

John had to put things into perspective: "Dear children, this is the last hour; and as you have heard that the antichrist is coming, even now many antichrists have come. This is how we know it is the last hour" (1 John 2:18).

Wonder how John tells time? "This," John says, "is the last hour." Two thousand years have slipped away since that "last hour." What time is it now?

John wasn't the only Bible writer who was certain he was living in the last hour. You get the same impression from Paul, Peter, and Jude. Of course, Peter also said: "But do not forget this one thing, dear friends: With the Lord a day is like a thousand years, and a thousand years are like a day" (2 Peter 3:8).

So I've heard people say that, applying Peter's clock-style, "It's only been two days since Jesus returned to heaven." But John wasn't thinking days or even hours. He said it is the *last* hour.

Obviously, It has been one *looong* hour. Obviously too, John was not referring to the 60-minute kind of hour. But as John looked ahead to the end of time and the return of Jesus Christ, he saw strong similarities between what *that* time would be like and what his own time was like. In fact, it was so similar that he viewed it all as the same time, the same "hour." What he didn't see then was that the "last hour" would stretch into hundreds of years.

You might say that, in John's mind, Christ's first and second comings collapsed together. Those two appearances of God's Son are what time is all about. The years between—even if there are thousands—are marking time in anticipation of history's climax.

Christians in Thessalonica were so sure Christ was returning immediately that the Apostle Paul had to clarify a few questions. "Don't let anyone deceive you in any way, for that day will not come until the rebellion occurs and the man of lawlessness is revealed, the man doomed to destruction. . . . And now you know what is holding him back, so that he may be revealed at the proper time" (2 Thessalonians 2:3, 6).

Peter put the delay into perspective. "The Lord is not slow in keeping His promise, as some understand slowness. He is patient with you, not wanting anyone to perish, but everyone to come to repentance" (2 Peter 3:9).

So, though it's been a long time and may be quite a while longer, John would still insist: "This is the last hour." And there was something about that last hour—*this* last hour—that disturbed John greatly.

Raising the Anti-

John, to whom the Book of Revelation was later given, saw that a person would one day come who would be the personification of everything Jesus Christ is opposed to. This person would stand *against* Christ, would put himself in the place of Christ. And if the reason for Christ's delay in returning is to give more people an opportunity to turn to Him, you would expect the *against-Christ* to be hell-bent on frustrating that purpose.

But what also bothered John was that the same against-Christ spirit was already alive and active. *The* Antichrist was coming, but *many* antichrists were already there. And these enemies who were coming *to* Christianity were, in another sense, also coming *from* Christianity.

"They went out from us, but they did not really belong to us. For if they had belonged to us, they would have remained with us; but their going showed that none of them belong to us" (1 John 2:19).

Cults and false teachings based on non-Christian philosophies and religions can be confusing. But even more confusing is a "new" religion that tosses in a dash of Jesus here and there! The biggest lies are not total lies; the biggest lies are mixtures of truth and error. Lots of truth—mmmm, the tasty appeal. Sometimes it takes a spiritual connoisseur to savor the difference. But spiritual connoisseurs are what we are to be.

Pour It On

How are we to taste the difference between truth and error? How can we be sure we're believing the truth? John gives a key word: *anointing*.

"But you have an anointing from the Holy One, and all of you know the truth. I do not write to you because you do not know the truth, but because you do know it and because no lie comes from the truth" (1 John 2:20-21).

The Jews were big on anointing. They poured oil on people as a sign of respect (Luke 7:46). They poured oil on people in preparation for burial (Mark 14:8). They also poured oil on people or things as a sign that they were dedicating them to God: the furniture in the tabernacle (Exodus 30:22-29), prophets (1 Kings 19:16), priests (Exodus 28:41), kings (2 Samuel 2:7). This ceremonial anointing of oil was a symbol of God's Holy Spirit.

When we read, "You have an anointing from the Holy One," we should visualize God pouring out His Spirit all over our lives—the same Spirit that was the force behind the authors of the Bible (2 Peter 1:21; 2 Timothy 3:16-17). John wrote what God's Spirit directed him to write. And that same Spirit, the Author of Truth, has become a guiding influence in our lives. We have been "anointed" with Him, and John says, "All of you know the truth" (1 John 2:20).

If true Christians have this anointing—are soaked with the Spirit oil of God—what about the antichrists? John's point seems harder for us to understand than it was for the original readers. They caught his suggestion immediately. The word "Christ" means "anointed one." To be antichrist, then, was to be anti-anointing.

These false teachers were standing against the anointing and anointed ones of God. They were putting themselves and their understanding in its place. They were resting on their wisdom, their knowledge, their so-called "enlightenment." In contrast, the Bible teaches: "I [God] will destroy the wisdom of the wise; the intelligence of the intelligent I will frustrate" (1 Corinthians 1:19).

But there's another point here. Notice that John puts all Christians on the same level. "All of you know the truth," he says. "I do not write to you because you do not know the truth, but because you do know it" (1 John 2:20-21). Most cults have a certain snob appeal. There are "those who are enlightened," and those who want to be; those who "know," and those who don't.

Christians can get caught up in this way of thinking too. Christian groups are often divided between the "really dedicated" people who know God, and the world-minded, pagan-influenced Christians who need to repent, be revived, or get fully committed. Once spiritually renewed, a member can be initiated into the inner circle.

Perhaps a few people in the group get concerned about their sin. They focus on their need to have some new experience with God. Maybe they get pushy or oppressive, figuring everyone has the same feelings or needs they do.

What happens? Others in the group feel threatened, left out. They haven't had the experience. And what should be good—someone getting closer to God—

instead becomes a damaging influence.

Though we can easily get caught up in things that take our attention away from God, though we may need to reexamine our commitment to Christ, the idea of a spiritual "caste system" is not a Christian concept at all. There are not insiders and outsiders in Christianity. There are not Christians who know the truth and Christians who don't.

We may need to know more. We may, like every other Christian in the world, need to keep growing. But every Christian knows the truth. We should beware of *any* religious group with an inner circle that people must struggle to be part of.

Crazy Splits

Churches and youth groups do the splits over the craziest things. One church couldn't agree on what kind of organ to buy.

"We need a Hammond," one person said.

"No, no, it should be a Rogers," another countered. "They sound just like pipe organs."

"I'm holding out for an Allen digital computer organ," someone else growled.

After bitter discussion and considerable hassle, the church finally agreed. But when the music director bought the organ, he ignored the group's decision and came back to the house of the Lord with a Wurlitzer. And predictably, the church was up in arms.

Dozens of issues divide Christians. Some of them are questions of how to understand the Bible. Some of the great dividers are nothing more than different ways to worship. Or what is or is not appropriate dress. Or what music style is right. Some of the biggest questions are really the silliest distinctions.

But there are certain things that a Christian cannot compromise without ceasing to be Christian. The dividing line is *Jesus*.

John expresses this point clearly: "Who is the liar? It is the man who denies that Jesus is the Christ. Such a man is the antichrist—he denies the Father and the Son. No one who denies the Son has the Father; whoever acknowledges the Son has the Father also" (1 John 2:22-23).

If you look at Jesus and don't see God, you have missed Christianity. If you deny Jesus as Christ, the Son of God, you also deny the Father, John says. You can't have one without the other. After all, who is Jesus? A moral teacher? A good man? A prophet? Plenty of cults and religious groups claim these titles for Jesus, but nothing more. The New Testament claims that He is much more:

"In the beginning was the Word, and the Word was with God, and the Word was God. He was with God in the beginning. Through Him all things were made; without Him nothing was made that has been made.... The Word became flesh and lived for a while among us. We have seen His glory, the glory of the one and only Son, who came from the Father, full of grace and truth" (John 1:1-3, 14).

"He [Christ] is the image of the invisible God, the firstborn over all creation. For by Him all things were created: things in heaven and on earth, visible and invisible, whether thrones or powers or rulers or authorities; all things were created by Him and for Him.

70 / New and Improved

He is before all things, and in Him all things hold together (Colossians 1:15-17).

Slipping Away

At one time the guitar-strumming cultists mentioned earlier were living together in an old building in downtown L.A. Since one of my college friends had a buddy, Steve, tangled up in the group, several of us decided to pay a visit. We hoped to speak with Steve and encourage him to return to his family.

It was a strange experience. We were greeted at the door by several "brothers." They had all taken biblical names like Ezekiel, Daniel, and Joshua. My friends and I waited, surrounded by "brothers" trying to argue us into the family, while someone went to get Steve.

When he joined us downstairs, the sight was pathetic. He was disheveled and spacy, but very determined. He had found love and acceptance, he said. He was also impressed at the amount of time cult members spent studying and witnessing. We finally left, feeling discouraged about Steve.

The cult leader, a former missionary, had drifted from the truth and had taken dozens of others with him. How? If the Son is the place of truth and security and He won't slip, how can we be sure *we* won't slip away from Him? What is our safeguard?

"See that what you have heard from the beginning remains in you. If it does, you also will remain in the Son and in the Father. And this is what He promised us—even eternal life" (1 John 2:24-25).

Remains ... remain. The Word *remains* in us. We

remain in the Son. But if we drift from the message, we drift from the Son. We don't carry on our relationship with Jesus in some odd and entirely mystical way. Instead, He gave a clear revelation; He wrote a book. As that message remains in us, we remain in Him.

The false teachers and cultists do just the opposite. They disregard the message. They drift away, perhaps slightly at first. But soon, instead of merely drifting, they are light-years away from what they once claimed to follow. And they take their followers with them into outer darkness.

"I am writing these things to you about those who are trying to lead you astray," John said. "As for you, the anointing you received from Him remains in you, and you do not need anyone to teach you. But as His anointing teaches you about all things and as that anointing is real, not counterfeit—just as it has taught you, remain in Him" (1 John 2:26-27).

What does it really mean to claim God as your Father? And what does He expect of His sons & daughters?

SIX

CHILD OF GOD, CHILD OF SATAN
1 John 2:28–3:10

You'd think it would all happen immediately. A person would become a Christian and *instantly* God would make him into everything He ever wanted him to become. This new Christian would *glow* spiritually. Next to this paragon of virtue, angels would blush at their comparative imperfection. Old habits would fall off like paper chains.

Even physically, the limitations would be forgotten as the new Christian surged with renewed health. No more sickness, suffering, or sorrow.

Everything this super-Christian prayed for would pop into reality: money, good times, friendship. He would pray for his grandma's brittle bones and they would become strong. He would pray for a job and without any further effort or initiative on his part, the job offers would roll in. All his obstacles would be effortlessly overcome; his enemies soundly defeated.

Life would be a breeze.

If we were designing the Christian system, it would probably go a lot like that. Becoming a Christian would activate some spiritual silicon chip, and with electron speed we'd become all we would *ever* become.

No struggles.
No questions.
No hassles.
No waiting.
No growth.

And no looking forward to what it means to become a full-grown child of God.

Slow to Make the "Seen"

The epitome of impatience is to pick up your favorite album, slip it on the turntable, but then anticipate each cut to the point that you don't enjoy what you're listening to. Perhaps you move the stylus to the next song before the previous tune is half finished.

All of life is being played out for all creation as if it is the one prime disc in God's collection. He knows what has come and what is coming, as if He can *hear* it all simultaneously; and, of course, He can. He *does*. And He likes the way it will all end—the final chorus. God has made life better, and will make it better still. All things will be brought to completion in Jesus Christ. But he lets the record play. He does not choose for the ending to stand independent of the rest of the production. Each detail plays its part.

God is patient. He doesn't mind waiting for things to unfold in their proper order. It is enough for each event, each age, each person, to have its perfectly timed appearing, its solo.

Do you ever wonder why He hasn't returned?

What will it be like to be with God?

Time will tell. Until then we are to enjoy the wait. But we're to wait *right*. And we don't have to wait to get instructions on how to wait.

Stay tuned as we pick up John's discussion of four *appearings* and what they mean for the person who says, "God is my Father."

Appearing #1: Jesus Christ will appear again. "And now, dear children, continue in Him, so that when He appears we may be confident and unashamed before Him at His coming" (1 John 2:28).

Surprise! Jesus is coming again. What's the surprise? A lot of people don't expect Him. And admittedly, He *has* been away quite a while now. Yet, people who *want* to expect His return have always accepted the Bible's word for it, regardless of how many years have come and gone. And people who do not want to believe it have always figured the whole idea was a hoax.

"They will say, 'Where is this coming He promised? Ever since our fathers died, everything goes on as it has since the beginning of creation'" (2 Peter 3:4).

The surprise for some people will be this: All their talk and speculation will prove to have been meaningless. John said, "*when* He appears," not "*if* He appears." And Jesus Himself promised, "If I go and prepare a place for you, I will come back and take you to be with Me that you also may be where I am" (John 14:3).

I'll take the word of John and Jesus, Peter and Paul.

Surprise? Here's another one: We may not have cleaned up our acts before the curtain call. John wants

76 / New and Improved

us to be *confident* and *unashamed* before Christ at His coming (1 John 2:28). What does that suggest? It's possible to be insecure and embarrassed at His coming.

The return of Jesus Christ is not going to be a glorified awards assembly in the sky, varsity letter and trophy for everybody. His coming is going to be the ultimate values sorter. When He comes, we will see in perspective what really matters in life—or should have mattered. Now we look at life and see a flat, two-dimensional sketch. When He returns, the picture will come to life. Depth and perspective will be added.

A life lived just for self will no longer appear to be "the good life"; we will see it for what it is. A rebellious, hateful life will no longer appear to be a life of justified hurt feelings; we will see it as it is. A life of squandered opportunities and wasted potential will no longer appear as simply "*my* life"; in that moment what it really was will shriek and scream.

The response will be profound shame.

But it doesn't have to be that way. The two-dimensional picture of life we have now is adequate, if we look carefully and honestly at our lives. We might say, as Paul did in another context, "If we judged ourselves, we would not come under judgment" (1 Corinthians 11:31). Paul was talking about the judgment and rebuke we might experience in this life as a result of persistent sin. John was talking about the sense of shame we might carry with us into Christ's presence. But we can avoid both kinds of pain.

How?

"Continue in Him," John says (1 John 2:28).

He had said that we are to watch out for false teachers, the *against-Christs*, by continuing in Christ and

Child of God, Child of Satan / 77

in the Word (1 John 2:24-27). Now John says that continuing in Him will also guard us from shame at His appearing. If our lives are wrapped up in Him now, it will seem natural to carry on that same relationship when we finally do see Him. Or to say it another way: Our close relationship with Jesus Christ is our link between this life and all it is to be, and our forever life with Him and all that it will be.

And how will *continuing in Him* express itself? By living like Him.

"If you know that He is righteous, you know that everyone who does what is right has been born of Him" (1 John 2:29).

I don't have to be paranoid about His return—*Will I be ashamed? Will I be ashamed?* If my life is right, my relationship with Him will be right.

Bionic Boots

"When Jesus Christ returns, what will happen to me? I'm not equipped for intergalactic travel." Good question. Complete answer impossible. But the partial answer introduces...

Appearing #2: What we're going to be. But first this necessary word of explanation: "How great is the love the Father has lavished on us, that we should be called children of God! And that is what we are! The reason the world does not know us is that it did not know Him" (1 John 3:1).

Catch the drift? The world does not recognize what we Christians really are. And there are times when we wonder ourselves. Maybe we are depressed, guilt-burdened, upset. We've just failed miserably and feel incredibly foolish. We've said we'd never lose our temper again but we've just nailed our kid sister, or mother, or best friend. We weren't going to give in to that temptation, "we had promised ourselves, and" we had promised God. But we crashed. Or we have big dreams and feel powerless. Or, maybe we feel adequate, together, relatively moral, yet we're aware that we are human, finite, limited, mortal.

But John says we are children of God.

Those words can easily be emptied of their meaning. Because we have heard the words for years, we can say, "Oh yes, children of God; kids of the kingdom. How cute. Nice of God to think up such a classy handle."

But we don't dare take the title "children of God" so lightly. God didn't intend it to be a quaint name tag. He wants us to know that He regards us as *His children*. God is our Father. Jesus Christ the Lord is our big brother.

"Both the One who makes men holy and those who are made holy are of the same family. So Jesus is not ashamed to call them brothers" (Hebrews 2:11).

People of the planet see us in a surface way. "Oh, there's Herman the religious fanatic" and "Mildred the Christian maniac." Or "the world" looks at us and sees nice people, friends perhaps. But *children of God*? How nervy! Audacious!

People of the planet looked at Jesus when He was here and said, "Oh, there's Joseph's boy, the religious fanatic" or "Jesus the maniac messiah." Others saw Him as a good carpenter, an intelligent and courteous boy, a friend, a teacher, a prophet. Few saw that He was the Son of God. If they missed that of *Him,* we shouldn't be too alarmed if they don't do cartwheels over our Christianity.

After all, what we are going to be hasn't appeared yet. "Dear friends, now we are children of God, and what we will be has not yet been made known. But we know that when He appears, we shall be like Him, for we shall see Him as He is" (1 John 3:2).

What will we be like when He returns? The answer is incomplete. But what we are told is enough. *We are going to be like Jesus.* Nobody knows all of what that will mean, but we have some insight.

After the Resurrection but before His return to the Father's right hand, Jesus was able to appear in a locked room, as if He stepped through the walls. Hmmm ... change in molecular structure? The physical details are secondary. Paul dismissed them by saying we now have a physical body; we are going to have a different body, a spiritual body. (Read all about it in 1 Corinthians 15.) But the greater fact is this: Our moral character is going to be transformed. We are going to be like Him!

Question: Why wait to get started?

"Everyone who has this hope in Him purifies himself, just as He is pure" (1 John 3:3).

Cliff Riding

I once heard a preacher talking about sin. It bothered him that people often asked if they could practice some questionable activity.

"People always want to know if it's OK to go to certain movies, to listen to degrading music. They al-

80 / New and Improved

ways want to know how much they can do before it is wrong."

We weren't quite following him, so he told the story of a trucking company who hired a new driver. It seems the boss told each applicant about a narrow mountain road, famous for its peril.

"How close can you drive your rig to the edge of the cliff before going over?" the boss then asked.

"Oh, couple of yards, I 'spect," said one man.

"I can bring them big wheels to within a few feet," said another.

And one man even boasted that he could roll his rig with his tires on the ledge.

Who got the job? The job went to a driver who answered, "Boy, I don't know. I always try to keep my semi as far away from a cliff as I can."

"That's how we should be with sin," the preacher concluded, "Not trying to see how close we can get to spiritual disaster, but how far we can stay away from it."

I've heard the same story from other preachers or youth speakers over the years. Sometimes it's truck drivers, sometimes stagecoach drivers. Always it's Christians. And the point is valid. The words *Christian* and *sin* ought to be mutually exclusive—they shouldn't go together. And that point introduces . . .

Appearing #3: Jesus appeared to wipe out sin. "Everyone who sins breaks the law; in fact, sin is lawlessness. But you know that He appeared so that He might take away our sins. And in Him is no sin. No one who lives in Him keeps on sinning. No one who continues to sin has either seen Him or known Him" (1 John 3:4-6).

When we become part of God's family, there has to be a change. The whole idea behind Christ's coming was to crush sin. How then can we become it's ally? "He has appeared once for all at the end of the ages to do away with sin by the sacrifice of Himself" (Hebrews 9:26). We can't toss our allegiance in with iniquity. We can't contradict what we are.

Show and Tell

As a young Christian, and a brand new high school graduate, I spent three weeks in intensive evangelism along Southern California's beaches. It was a summer outreach effort involving about a dozen college students, an elderly couple, and me.

I was the youngest student and the newest Christian. And since we lived together in a large beach house, I had ample opportunity to see how "mature Christians" lived. I found it fascinating! They smiled. They laughed. They cried. They made mistakes—sometimes admitting them, sometimes covering them up. And they prayed.

I was especially interested in their praying, since I was new to this whole Christian thing. I listened hard when they prayed. They sounded like they were talking to God or something. And, of course, they were. But I found myself making mental notes of certain words and phrases these brothers and sisters used so that I could use them in my own prayers.

I soon learned that I could punctuate someone else's prayers with a string of well-placed "amens" and "yes, Lords." When I got the system down, I suddenly felt very Christian.

Then it happened.

I sound like a child of God, I caught myself thinking one afternoon as I prayed with one of the other guys. As he prayed, I laid it on thick. I had my "amens" and "yes, Lords" going full steam.

Then I prayed. And I prayed and prayed and prayed. But something wasn't quite right. I couldn't hear my friend's "amens" and "yes, Lords." Was I getting through? Finally, I stopped mid-sentence and opened my eyes. Stan was asleep.

Why pray, I thought, *no one's listening anyway.* I got up, walked into the other room, sat down on the couch, picked up my guitar and *wham*!—the truth hit me! *Who have I been praying to? How have I been gauging my spirituality? What makes me feel so close to God?*

There *is* a way to know and "feel" you are a child of God, but it goes much deeper than words. John expresses it as . . .

Appearing #4: What we really are inside shows. "Dear children, do not let anyone lead you astray. He who does what is right is righteous, just as He is righteous. He who does what is sinful is of the devil, because the devil has been sinning from the beginning. The reason the Son of God appeared was to destroy the devil's work. No one who is born of God will continue to sin, because God's seed remains in Him; he cannot go on sinning, because he has been born of God" (1 John 3:7-9).

And in case we are missing the point, John spells it out: "This is how we know who the children of God are and who the children of the devil are. Anyone who does not do what is right is not a child of God; neither is anyone who does not love his brother" (1 John 3:10).

John paints the picture in broad stokes, clear for everyone to see: If you continually live like the devil, you're not a child of God. Sin is not one of God's traits, and children will look like their fathers.

Of course a child of God *can* sin, and does. But John is saying that someone who is born into God's family won't continue in his same old, sinful way of living. A real change takes place. He may stumble and fall, but he is headed in a different direction than before.

"God can make your life better," we can imagine John saying, and then pressing the point, "Is it?"

What guides my life?
What makes me do
 what I do,
say what I say,
 think what I think?

SEVEN

LOVE IN TRUTH, LOVE IN ACTION
1 John 3:11-24

What bothers Steve is the question of motives. Always there are people ready to tell him what he should be doing, and how he should be doing it. If he does not measure up, the guilt is inescapable. And Steve can't shake one nagging question: Why?

People expect him to share his faith?

Why?

He is to respect authority figures.

Why?

No sex before marriage.

Why?

Read the Bible. Pray. Go to church.

Why? Why? *Why?*

If you're the one being asked why, it can be an enormously bothersome question. After all, if the expectations are good ones, like the ones above (praying, going to church), why ask why?

86 / New and Improved

Why?

My four-year-old son hitches a question-caboose on every train of thought that rumbles past him. And his favorite question is, "Why?" Why he likes the question, I don't know, but I have a feelng it's good that he asks. At least he's conscious—learning and growing.

Question: Why do people outgrow the healthy habit of asking why? We feel pressed by our peers into something we may not even like. And we go along with it without so much as a three-letter question: *Why?*

Our world is reeling from critical problems, yet many people don't seem to care. Why? Because they bounce along the surface of life without thinking deeply, without asking the cosmic question, *Why?* And to the people who have the good sense to ask the obvious questions, others ask, "Why ask? What's wrong with him?"

Yet, as I sit here, trying to make sense of the Apostle John's letter, my mind keeps turning to my friend Steve. Why? Because Steve is asking the *why* question not only about life's negatives, but also about its positives. He knows it's not enough that something seems right; that's not always reason enough to do it. The deeper question is. *Why do it? What motivates me?*

And the Answer Is . . .

Why is a question the New Testament asks repeatedly. Christianity does not demand of us mere obedience. It demands that the why behind our obedience be the right why.

It's not that we can never obey God unless we

understand all the reasons. We should do what we know to be right, because we know it's right. But still there is the question of motives—the why? And ultimately, the why is *love.*

Step closer and see.

"This is the message you heard from the beginning: We should love one another" (1 John 3:11).

No surprise there. John has already said: "Anyone who claims to be in the light but hates his brother is still in the darkness. Whoever loves his brother lives in the light, and there is nothing in him to make him stumble" (1 John 2:9-10).

And John has already told us what we are not to love. "Do not love the world or anything in the world" (1 John 2:15).

Now John picks up the subject of love again, and after a brief interruption (1 John 4:1-6), he will again return to the theme. John keeps coming back to the subject of love because love is foundational. Love is the *why* that all of Christianity hangs on. Love, said Jesus, is the greatest of the commandments (Matthew 22:34-40). So John insists: *We must love, and we must understand what love is not* (1 John 3:11-15).

"Do not be like Cain, who belonged to the evil one and murdered his brother. And why did he murder him? Because his own actions were evil and his brother's were righteous" (1 John 3:12).

John's comments point back to Genesis 4 and the story of the first murder. It's an odd story. Cain was a farmer, Abel a herdsman. Each was to bring a sacrifice to God. It was to be a "blood sacrifice," one that looked forward to the ultimate, all-time sacrifice which would take away the guilt of sin—Jesus Christ. Abel brought a lamb. Cain brought veggies. And God accepted Abel's sacrifice, but was displeased with Cain's.

Cain was angry, brooding. And God said to him: "Why are you angry? Why is your face downcast? If you do what is right, will you not be accepted? But if you do not do what is right, sin is crouching at your door; it desires to have you, but you must master it" (Genesis 4:6-7).

At this point, Cain's solution was simple. He knew what was right and, if he did it, God promised to accept him. But Cain ignored God's counsel, threw his spirit open to his anger and temptation, and murdered his younger brother.

Catch the force of Cain's crime. There had never been a murder before. Murder wasn't a part of everyday life—cheap TV shows, sleazy novels, and the evening news—as it is today. Murder was born in Cain's mind. He listened to his natural inclinations, his pride, his jealousy.

Love defeats these things. Love recognizes that natural inclinations, unaided by God's Spirit, will destroy us and others. Love sees that pride must die in preference to the needs and concerns of others. Love sees jealousy for the destructive force that it is.

"Do not be surprised, my brothers, if the world hates you. We know that we have passed from death to life, because we love our brothers. Anyone who does not love remains in death" (1 John 3:13-14).

What is John telling us? Why does he say these things? What are we to understand about the nature of love?

Real love is alien. It invaded the planet through Jesus Christ. In Jesus, God demonstrated an entirely different class of love (Romans 5:8). Unconditional, "no-matter-what" love. Self-sacrificing love.

The people of the planet do not understand this kind of love. And they do not understand us.

What could be greater proof of new life than to have this kind of love working in us? We know that we have stepped out of the realm of death and into the kingdom of life ... if love characterizes us, motivates us.

And if it doesn't?

John leaves no middle ground. He puts constructive love in opposition to destructive hate. And he equates hate with murder.

"Anyone who hates his brother is a murderer, and you know that no murderer has eternal life in him" (1 John 3:15).

To Take, To Give

After explaining what love is not, John tells us what love is. "This is how we know what love is: Jesus Christ laid down His life for us. And we ought to lay down our lives for our brothers" (1 John 3:16).

Hate takes.

Love gives.

Prime example: Jesus.

We might be tempted to ask, "How can my love be expressed then? I probably will not have opportunity to give my life." So John clarifies. Love gives whatever is needed. It blushes at the idea of holding back. It sees a need and moves to meet it. It gladly gives up its resources.

"If anyone has material possessions and sees his brother in need but has no pity on him, how can the love of God be in him? Dear children, let us not love with words or tongue but with actions and in truth" (1 John 3:17-18).

What do these verses say to us as Christians as we consider a world of hungry people? And what do they say about the person next door or across the aisle in history class who needs our concern? Our love?

I remember a high school classmate who, for some weird reason, was not considered part of our inner circle. He was quiet, and not particularly gross in his behavior. Maybe that was the problem. Maybe he was too good, too nice for our friendship.

Then too he played the accordion. That seemed odd. Accordions didn't have strings and tuning pegs. You couldn't strum an accordion, or pick one either. So there was Jerry on the outer fringes of friendship. But he was always nice to me.

If my lunch was unexciting, as it often was, Jerry was the guy who gladly shared. He brought the neatest things. He sat and listened to me, or carried on a relaxed conversation.

But as I established friendships with other people, I found I had less time for Jerry. Before long, I was eating lunch with other friends and seldom even thought of Jerry. I hadn't decided to drop him from my friendship roster, it just happened. But it happened easily.

Then one afternoon—I don't even remember why—I was walking down the hallway during the lunch hour. Our Southern California high school had a large plaza. Most people who brought their lunch ate in that area. There were a few other places around campus where others ate. But along this hallway adjoining a row of classrooms, no one ate. Not one single person. Except Jerry.

I looked down this long strip of cement and there was nothing, but Jerry. This whole section of the school was virtually deserted. As I walked by, I looked down at Jerry, leaning against the building. And I thought, *I have never seen a guy who looked so lonely.* But I kept walking.

Today, as I reflect on that and then consider what John says about love, I feel awkward, guilty. God's love in us ought to cut across all the cliques and silly social barriers.

And I think of my family. I now live 2,000 miles from them. When I was younger, there was a time when we almost seemed strangers to one another; a time when we were more aware of our differences and problems. Now, in spite of the distance, I feel very close to them. But I remember that time, and I read John's words, and they haunt me:

"Dear children, let us not love with words or tongue but with actions and in truth" (1 John 3:18).

Heart to Heart

"This then is how we know that we belong to the truth, and how we set our hearts at rest in His presence whenever our hearts condemn us. For God is greater than our hearts, and He knows everything" (1 John 3:19-20).

John here makes an abrupt shift—from our responsibility to love one another, to the health of our relationship with God: If we love, we know that we belong to the truth (v. 19). If we love, our hearts rest in His presence (vv. 19-20). In the verses that follow, John expands on the love/God connection. And he insists: *We must love, and here's what that love will accomplish....*

"Dear friends, if our hearts do not condemn us, we have confidence before God and receive from Him anything we ask, because we obey His commands and do what pleases Him. And this is His command: to believe in the name of His Son, Jesus Christ, and to love one another as He commanded us. Those who obey His commands live in Him, and He in them. And this is how we know that He lives in us: We know it by the Spirit He gave us" (1 John 3:21-24).

Again John links obeying God's commands with loving one another. But He also links it with something else. He says it's our love-obedience that lets us rest in our relationship with God. Love-obedience gives us confidence (1 John 3:21).

Remember Steve, the "why guy"? The problem with Steve is that he can't satisfy his mind that in God the questions are all satisfactorily resolved. Steve seems convinced that all his questions are ultimately answered in Jesus Christ, but he's not convinced he will be thrilled with the outcome.

"I'm afraid of God," he tells me. "And I get all these guilt trips laid on me about what I should do or be. But why? Why does this fear thing have to motivate it all? Why must I obey God or else? Where's love in all this?"

I want to scream, "Love is the core, Steve!" Instead,

I wait. I wait and listen. I need to hear the frustration he feels.

And I can't fight off the feeling that we Christians contribute to Steve's confusion. It's so easy to misrepresent God. Steve is partially right. You can't do the right things for the wrong reasons and then expect God to be thrilled. That can degenerate into legalism and hypocrisy. But there's freedom in love, liberty in obedience. Steve needs to be reminded that God is greater than his heart, because Steve's heart condemns him too much.

"If our hearts do not condemn us, we have confidence before God" (1 John 3:21). If our relationship with God is right, we don't have to fear.

With this confidence-before-God verse, John again returns to a theme he's presented before. He looks ahead to Christ's second coming: "And now, dear children, continue in Him, so that when He appears we may be confident and unashamed before Him at His coming" (1 John 2:28).

Continue in love.
Continue in Him.
Be confident.

Next, John points out that love-obedience sparks prayer too. As we "continue in Him": "We have confidence before God and receive from Him anything we ask, because we obey His commands and do what pleases Him" (1 John 3:21-22).

Two things are triggered by obedience: (1) We feel more confident in asking because we have a keener sense as to what we ought to request. (2) Our obedience, in some sense, releases God's response to our prayers.

Sign on the Dotted Line

From time to time I've tried to figure out why I wasted several years between the time of my vague religious commitment and my reevaluation of that agreement I made with God. Was the problem that I did not understand Christianity? Partly. But mainly it was that Christians I knew tried to make the faith far too easy.

"Simply ask Jesus into your life and He really will come in."

"Christ will give you an abundant life."

"Go forward."

"Sign here."

"Say yes."

"Open the door."

It is hard to complicate the easy word *believe*. But the word believe is not easy. I cannot toss God token faith then live life in a business-as-usual way. Faith makes bold demands of me ... if it is truly faith. Faith stirs me out of ho-hum presumption. Faith crushes complacency.

Example: "This is His command: to believe in the name of His Son, Jesus Christ, and to love one another as He commanded us. Those who obey His commands live in Him, and He in them" (1 John 3:23-24).

See the word with the hook in it, the word you just cannot breeze over?

"This is His *command*."

"As He *commanded* us."

"Obey His *commands*."

But the other action words in these verses fill in the rest of the picture:

"*Believe* and *love*."

"*Obey* and *live.*"

Steve's *why* is an OK question. Some people ought to ask it more often. But when it comes to Christianity, he is stumbling over the essence of what it means to *believe.* Love motivates us, but the expectations are high. When God designed His better way of life, He built it on the balance of belief and love, obedience and life. And it's not our place to cheapen those high demands.

*Don't we snag our religion
on the horns of a dilemma
if we say that only Christianity
has the truth,
only Christians really love?*

EIGHT

SPIRIT OF TRUTH, SPIRIT OF ERROR
1 John 4:1-6

What irritated Ron as much as anything was the idea that "the only way to God is through Jesus." Ron could accept the value of Christianity; he could appreciate the teachings of Jesus. But the idea that there was no other way to find God ... that was just too much to swallow.

How could anyone be so egotistical as to claim a religious monopoly?—"If you want to live forever, you better buy your celestial real estate from me."

Another thing that irked Ron was to hear believers talk as if only Christians knew anything about peace and joy. That's not to say that Ron was particularly peaceful or joyful. He wasn't either. But he knew people who rejected Christianity without becoming as miserable as Christians said they would become. Besides, to be told that, apart from Jesus, life was hopeless seemed hopelessly narrow and bigoted.

98 / New and Improved

Ron had a point. And so did the Christians.

Some non-Christians are happy, and there is some truth in other religions. If non-Christian religions were *completely* wrong, it's doubtful they would have so many followers! Many religions teach some of the same ideas as Christianity. Good ideas. God, you might say, did not choose to hide all truth from the non-Christians.

People who study theology toss around the phrase "common grace." By it they mean that God, in His goodness, extends many of His gifts to the entire world. You don't have to be His official, born-again child to benefit.

Ron is right too about some Christians. We are often careless in the way we present Christ. He did not promise to lift all our cares and trim our spiritual sails so we could cruise through a problem-free life. In fact, the night before His death, Jesus, told His disciples that things were going to be tough. Then He added, "I have told you these things, so that in Me you may have peace. In this world you will have trouble. But take heart! I have overcome the world" (John 16:33).

Furthermore, Ron would add, some Christians are hypocritical, inconsistent. It's not unusual to run into a non-Christian who is more *moral* than many Christians. To the casual observer, the idea that only Christians are "together" is absurd.

So we Christians are in an awkward position. We don't have a corner on morality, truth, or happiness. Yet Jesus said plainly, "I am the way and the truth and the life. No man comes to the Father except through Me. If you really knew Me, you would know My Father as well. From now on, you do know Him and have seen Him" (John 14:6-7).

On with the Dilemma

In 1 John 3:11-24, John talks about love. In 1 John 4:7-21, John talks about love again. Sandwiched between these two love-talks are six verses about false teachers, antichrists, and the spirit of error.

Question: Why interrupt a perfectly good love-talk, John? The answer is: We Christians have a dilemma!

Consider: In 1 John 3:11-15, John draws a contrast between love and hate. And he insists that we know we have passed from death to life because we love. The presence of love in our lives shouts to the world that something supernatural has happened to us, something that hasn't happened to the people in the world.

But wouldn't some non-Christian wonder, *Where do these Christians get off saying I don't love?*

In 1 John 3:16-19, John explains that the death of Jesus gave love meaning. We learn what love is through Him.

But non-Christians protest, "I don't believe in Jesus, but I do understand love."

In 1 John 3:19-24, John relates our life of love to a right relationship with God. If love lives in us—His love—we don't have to be afraid in God's presence. Prayers get answered. We know for sure we are close to Him.

But non-Christians argue, "I know what it means to love, but I'm not sure I ever want to be close to your God!"

See the dilemma?

To make matters worse, we have the problem of "false teachers." They might misrepresent the truths in 1 John and make the issues even more unclear: If God is love, why not say love is God since the only thing that matters is love?

Aware of the possibility of being read wrong, God's Spirit directed John to clarify: "Dear friends, do not believe every spirit, but test the spirits to see whether they are from God, because many false prophets have gone out into the world" (1 John 4:1).

John has already urged us to rely on the anointing we have from God's Spirit (1 John 2:20-21). John has said that all true Christians know truth. And he has told us that a false teacher is someone who denies that Jesus is the Christ, God's sent Son (vv. 22-23). John has said we should resist false teaching by hanging onto the Word (vv. 24-27). Now he turns the coin to inspect it from a different angle.

Christians are given the Spirit, John reminds us; the anointing is from Him. God's Spirit is the guarantee that we know God. "This is how we know that [God] lives in us: We know it by the Spirit He gave us" (1 John 3:24). By *that* Spirit, we test *all* spirits.

True-False Test

Why John's concern about false teaching? For years Christians did not have a completed Bible. They couldn't pick up a well-worn New Testament and compare God's Word with what some preacher said, just to be sure.

The New Testament books and letters, including 1 John, were widely circulated and, as we know, were eventually bound together in Bible form. But until then, Christians relied on the apostles and prophets to reveal God's thoughts, His new truth. So it was important for Christians to know that God's Spirit, living in them, would be their teacher (2:27). Through Him they could test other spirits.

As for prophets, what was to keep them from claiming that the true spirit gave them a message, when actually they had dreamed it up or an evil spirit had given it to them?

False prophets were common in Old Testament times, and God had told His people to test their messages. How? "If what a prophet proclaims in the name of the Lord does not take place or come true, that is a message the Lord has not spoken. That prophet has spoken presumptuously. Do not be afraid of him" (Deuteronomy 18:22).

"If a prophet, or one who foretells by dreams, appears among you and announces to you a miraculous sign or wonder, and if the sign or wonder of which he has spoken takes place, and he says, 'Let us follow other gods' (gods you have not known) 'and let us worship them,' you must not listen to the words of that prophet or dreamer. The Lord your God is testing you to find out whether you love Him with all your heart and with all your soul. It is the Lord your God you must follow, and Him you must revere. Keep His commands and obey Him; serve Him and hold fast to Him" (Deuteronomy 13:1-4).

In 1 Corinthians 12, the Apostle Paul deals with this same "false prophet" problem: "You know that when you were pagans, somehow or other you were influenced and led astray to dumb idols. Therefore I tell you that no one who is speaking by the Spirit of God says, 'Jesus be cursed,' and no one can say, 'Jesus is Lord,' except by the Holy Spirit" (1 Corinthians 12:2-3).

Jesus is the true-false test. John says the same thing: "This is how you can recognize the Spirit of God: Every spirit that acknowledges that Jesus Christ has come in the flesh is from God, but every spirit that does not acknowledge Jesus is not from God. This is the spirit of the antichrist, which you have heard is coming and even now is already in the world" (1 John 4:2-3).

Just a Man?

So we're back to the dilemma of "the narrow way" and my frustrated, unbelieving friend Ron. Ron enjoyed a good argument as much for the sake of an argument as anything else. Don't get the impression that he was a spiritual seeker, hunting for truth. Instead, picture Ron as angry.

Ron had a bad temper. And nothing set him off quite like "religion." You could trace the progression of his anger by the twisted thread of his thoughts. He would ask questions such as: "Can God make a stone so big He can't pick it up?"

Ponder that. And assuming you were to dignify it with an answer, what would you say?

"Why yes, of course."

"Then He's not really God if He can't even lift a stone!"

"Er, no, of course He *can't.*"

"Then He's not God. I thought God could do *anything*!"

The point is, Ron started out logically, asking some reasonable questions. But the longer he talked, the madder he got, and the madder he got, the more irrational he became.

"Without faith it is impossible to please God, because anyone who comes to Him must believe that He exists and that He rewards those who earnestly seek Him" (Hebrews 11:6).

"Without faith it is impossible to please God." And in Ron's case we might add: "Without faith it is impossible to please yourself." There may be some people without God who are not restless and frustrated. But Ron wasn't one of them.

And yet when I think of Ron's irrational question, "Can God make a stone so big He can't pick it up?" I realize that the truth is nearly that "irrational":

"Can God be both *God* and *man* at the same time?"

"Can God die?"

"Can the sacrifice of a God-man erase the guilt of immoral people?"

The Apostle Paul says bluntly, "The message of the Cross is foolishness to those who are perishing, but to us who are being saved it is the power of God" (1 Corinthians 1:18).

Is it really surprising then that false teachers stumble over the issue of who Jesus is? God's logic is so alien to this world that it appears irrational.

A popular false teaching in John's day was the notion, common today, that Jesus was merely a man. A *good* man. But *just* a man. Then something happened, this false teaching claimed. When John the Baptist baptized Jesus, "godness" fell on Him—He became divine, special, but not special in a unique sense really, just special. When "godness" saw that Jesus was faltering in the polls, it made its exit, leaving a just-human Jesus to die. After all, the false teachers reasoned, how could *God* die?

These teachers refused to bring the *humanness* of Jesus and the *godness* of Jesus together. God could be God. Man could be man. But the two could not be mixed.

They looked at man's spirit, or soul, and said: "Good stuff." They looked at the body, or anything physical, and said: "Rot!" So they stroked their souls, and denied their bodies. Or they figured their bodies were so unimportant that they might as well do whatever they pleased! Some of this group were extreme in their self-denial; others were extreme in their cruddy living.

But Christianity put body and soul in balance. And the God-man Jesus was the prime example. He remained fully God and fully human, yet He died. The seemingly irrational is truth. Believe it! Then test the spirits.

Foolish Questions?

As a result of my talks with Ron and others, I have adopted a motto: "Any fool can ask a question a thousand wise men can't answer."

Fact is, I embraced that proverb largely out of self-defense. I believed Jesus. Christianity seemed logical enough, in a divinely irrational way. I knew you could become a Christian without assassinating your brain. But still there were scores of questions seemingly with no answers.

Sometimes I still feel guilty when a non-Christian confronts me with a religious question I can't find a good answer for. But in my saner moments I realize that God can defend His own honor. I don't have to protect Him. My task is to achieve that balance of holding onto what I know is true, while facing honest questions honestly.

Now think of the Christians John was writing to. They did not have a completed Bible. They did not have a whole library of Christian books to help them explore the fine points. They couldn't always run to an apostle with their questions. But what does John say to them?

"You, dear children, are from God and have overcome them, because the One who is in you is greater than the one who is in the world" (1 John 4:4).

The false teachers enjoyed being philosophical and academic. They were eloquent. Not every Christian would have been capable of refuting every specific argument.

When John says, "You have overcome them," he's not thinking of some kind of great debate. John's point is, "You didn't sell out the truth just because someone threw some teachings at you that you didn't understand."

Some people fall because they are not willing to say, "I don't know." The arguments sound convincing, so they accept them rather than look like a jerk. Pride brings them down.

A better response is to say, "I just don't know about that, but I know this: Jesus is Lord." It's not worth sacrificing what we know to be true for the sake of salvaging our intellectual respect.

Moral Minority

Let's face it: As Christians, we are the "moral minority." Christianity is not the majority opinion. John said of the antichrists: "They are from the world and therefore speak from the viewpoint of the world, and the world listens to them" (1 John 4:5).

Since these false teachers are, as John says "from the world," you would expect them to "speak from the viewpoint of the world." Christian truth is not something you come to *naturally*. Paul has the same conflict in mind when he writes:

The man without the Spirit does not accept the things that come from the Spirit of God, for they are foolishness to him, and he cannot understand them, because they are spiritually discerned" (1 Corinthians 2:14).

All of which brings us full circle to our Christian dilemma—the question of a religious monopoly. Can we say that the Christian way—the Jesus way—is the only way?

Peter said it: "Salvation is found in no one else, for there is no other name under heaven given to men by which we must be saved" (Acts 4:12).

Paul said it: "Therefore God exalted Him [Jesus] to the highest place and gave Him the name that is above every name, that at the name of Jesus every knee should bow, in heaven and on earth and under the earth, and every tongue confess that Jesus Christ is Lord, to the glory of God the Father" (Philippians 2:9-11).

Jesus said it: "I am the way and the truth and the life. No man comes to the Father except through Me"

(John 14:6).

Can we compassionately, humbly say it? Christianity is unique. Some philosophy, some religion may improve your life. But God can make it better still, because Christianity is truth.

"We are from God," John says unapologetically, "and whoever knows God listens to us; but whoever is not from God does not listen to us. This is how we recognize the Spirit of Truth and the spirit of falsehood" (1 John 4:6).

If love is so prominent, if it's the centerpiece of Christianity, how can we experience it, understand it, share it?

NINE

LIVE IN LOVE, LIVE IN GOD
1 John 4:7-21

Most of us have a hard time understanding unconditional love, simply because we don't have much firsthand experience of it. We know how to love someone for what we can weasel out of him. And we know how to swap loving feelings in exchange for loving feelings. But usually, buried somewhere deep in us is the question:

Would he love me if...?

Or: *Does she just love me because...?*

Another reason we find it difficult to understand unconditional love is because we have a hard time loving ourselves. Most of us have things about ourselves that we're embarrassed by or ashamed of. Since we don't fully accept ourselves, we can't believe anyone else could fully accept us either—if they knew us as we really are.

Feeling loved is a strange sensation, hard to get used

to. And the hardest thing about love may simply be accepting it, opening ourselves up to the *risk* of receiving it.

Receiving love is a risk because most of us have been hurt by love—by a parent that disappointed us, a boyfriend or girlfriend that traded us in on a new affection, a friend who betrayed us. The risk of love is that we might keep transmitting it while the other person stops receiving it and tunes in another station. Because of our fears and frustrations, most of us are just not prepared for real love when we stumble across it.

But Christianity runs boldly into the middle of our questions and fears—and offers a new way to love.

Run That by Me Again

Maybe you have noticed that John returns to certain themes again and again in his letter. He has discussed false teachers twice already (1 John 2:18-27 and 4:1-6). He has hit sin a couple of times (1:5—2:2 and 3:4-10). And the subject of love has also found its way into John's letters more than once (2:9-11 and 3:11-24).

It's not that elderly John sat down to write, then dropped his notes on the floor. He repeats these themes on purpose.

We are used to people thinking, writing, and talking linearly. They begin with their first point, move on to their second, then their third and fourth, etc. They write in one long, straight line. If they were writing 1 John they would say everything they had to say about love, then move on to sin, and from there to prayer.

But John wrote *cyclically*—in cycles. In a good sense, he talked in circles. He talked about sin and then love and then prayer. Then he tilted the discussion the other way, thought about it from another perspective, and gave it another whirl. Each time a topic popped up again, John gave it new insight.

1 John's cyclical structure reminds me of Christianity itself. I don't arrive at an understanding of *the Holy Spirit*, then move on to *sin*, and from there to *love*, taking the full dose of each. Instead, I am constantly learning and relearning. I face an experience and gain new understanding from it, but a year or a day later, I am learning it again.

We might be tempted to discuss a topic and then dispose of it. But John won't permit that. So now he brings *love* back for another orbit, and as he does, he shares *four big ideas about love.*

Big idea #1: Love makes the invisible God visible.

"Dear friends, let us love one another, for love comes from God. Everyone who loves has been born of God and knows God" (1 John 4:7).

The opposite is true too: "Whoever does not love does not know God, because God is love" (1 John 4:8).

It's impossible to separate knowing God from loving people. The reason is that God's very identity is wrapped up in love: "God is love" (1 John 4:16).

The idea of God entering my life and not coloring my relationships with love is unthinkable. Love comes from God. If God shares my life, love has to come from me too.

And how does love behave? "This is how God showed His love among us: He sent His one and only

> Four big ideas:
>
> #1 Love makes the invisible God visible.
>
> #2 We can count on God's love.
>
> #3 Love gets rid of fear.
>
> #4 Love for God demands love for others.

Son into the world that we might live through Him. This is love: not that we loved God, but that He loved us and sent His Son as an atoning sacrifice for our sins" (1 John 4:9-10).

Note that it is not our love for God that makes love understandable. It is God's love for us. Can we really say that our love for God is unselfish? Can we honestly say that we don't love God for what He gives *us*?

If we knew that God was sending us to hell because

we earned it, and yet we walked into hell loving God freely, then we might begin to grasp unselfish love. In a real sense, when Jesus Christ stretched out on the cross as our substitute, when God poured all our sin on Him, He went to hell for us. And all the while, He loved us and the Father freely. There is no greater expression of love.

Me? Love Them?

Realize: Christianity is not some cheap, bargain-basement religion. Christ makes awesome demands of us. "Dear friends," John continues, "since God so loved us, we also ought to love one another" (1 John 4:11).

Picture this: God. Holy. Perfect. Totally independent. He needs nothing. No one. But He decides to love us.

We are scuzzy. Unworthy. Hideously sinful, compared to God (and that's who we're supposed to compare ourselves to). We are so dependent on the day-to-day goodness of God that without Him we would self-destruct.

And *God* loves *us*?

And God *loves* us!

So, we step into Christianity dazed at that love. We look at Jesus on the cross and begin to understand unconditional love. Then God comes to us and says, "Love one another."

And we protest. "But God, love my parents? After the way they hurt me?" Or, "Love that lonely person? He's so odd and out-of-it."

Jesus persists. "Love your enemies and pray for those who persecute you, that you may be sons of your

Father in heaven" (Matthew 5:44-45).

"But they're scuzzy, unworthy, hideously sinful!"

"So were you," God reminds us.

And something happens when we do love. We make the invisible God visible. "No one has ever seen God; but if we love each other, God lives in us and His love is made complete in us" (1 John 4:12).

Christians loving unconditionally is the closest thing most people get to seeing God. It may even introduce them to...

Big idea #2: We can rely on God's love.

"We know that we live in Him and He in us, because He has given us of His Spirit. And we have seen and testify that the Father has sent His Son to be the Saviour of the world. If anyone acknowledges that Jesus is the Son of God, God lives in Him and He in God. And so we know and rely on the love God has for us" (1 John 4:13-16).

Maybe Today

I remember sitting in a church service with three other youth group members. When the pastor started discussing sin and Christ's return, a friend glanced over and rolled his eyeballs as if to say, "Here it comes again."

Then, to get his point across, the pastor said: "You want to know whether something is sinful? Ask yourself how you would feel if you were involved in that activity when Christ returned. What if you were at that place you shouldn't be, and Christ was suddenly there?"

My friends and I looked at one another as if to say, "Good point, Preacher! You really nailed us on that one!"

I could see myself sinning and then suddenly staring Jesus in the face, stammering out a flimsy excuse. I could see it. And I didn't like it.

In time, through God's grace, I got my life together. I stepped into Christianity dazed by God's *love*. And I forgot the preacher's illustration. Now I was *looking forward* to Christ's return. It didn't occur to me that I should fear it.

Years later, while reading 1 John, I stumbled on a verse that shed a different light on the matter: "Dear children, continue in Him, so that when He appears we may be confident and unashamed before Him at His coming" (1 John 2:28).

Oh yeah, I reminded myself, *I'm supposed to be scared of Jesus, nervous about His return.* And I thought about that. No, that didn't sound quite right either. But on the other hand. . . .

I continued reading in 1 John, determined to sort out the fear question sooner or later. I didn't have to wait long. Fortunately for me, John wrote in circles rather than lines and—*zap!*—I hit chapter 4 and tripped over the same concept. This time around, John handled the fear factor from a different perspective.

Fear Factor

What I ran across in 1 John had something to do with Christ's return. It had something to do with fear. It had everything to do with love.

116 / New and Improved

Big idea #3: Love gives fear the boot.

"God is love. Whoever lives in love lives in God, and God in him. Love is made complete among us so that we will have confidence on the day of judgment, because in this world we are like Him. There is no fear in love. But perfect love drives out fear, because fear has to do with punishment. The man who fears is not made perfect in love" (1 John 4:16-18).

There it was—conclusive proof, in black and white, that I didn't have to fear God. Moreover, I was to look with confidence toward Christ's return. There's no fear in love. Love puts fear out to pasture.

Why can we have confidence before God? Remember: He is holy, perfect, independent; we are something else again. What's going to happen when Christ returns? We are going to see Him, live in Him. But if His love lives in us, the big changes in our lives begin now. "God is love. Whoever lives in love lives in God, and God in Him" (1 John 4:16). Seeing Christ is not a fearful surprise. We can have confidence, "because in this world we are like Him" (v. 17).

Why fear meeting God if you are *like Him*? What on earth is going to upset Him—if you are like Him, if you live in love?

Love is a liberating thing; it drives out fear. But it's not liberating because it *overlooks* moral crud. It's liberating because it *overcomes* moral crud—defeats it, scours it into holiness.

But here is the other side of that good news. Some people *should* have a healthy dose of fear. John says, "The man who fears is not made perfect in love." But that man's problem is not that he needs to shake his fear; rather he needs to live in Christ's love. In other words, the man who fears is not made perfect in love; but the man who is not made perfect in love may need to fear.

Example: "Not everyone who says to Me, 'Lord, Lord,' will enter the kingdom of heaven, but only he who does the will of My Father who is in heaven" (Matthew 7:21).

We need to be sure we are part of God's family.

"We must pay more careful attention, therefore, to what we have heard, so that we do not drift away. For if the message spoken by angels was binding, and every violation and disobedience received its just punishment, how shall we escape if we ignore such a great salvation?" (Hebrews 2:1-3)

Fear that merely leads to more fear accomplishes nothing. Instead, God challenges us to live in His love and watch our fears dissolve!

Blind Love?

Ugandan Bishop Festo Kivengere shocked the world by writing the book, *I Love Idi Amin*. Amin was the ruthless military dictator who had savagely persecuted the Christians in that African country. He had slaughtered them. Even Kivengere had to flee the country for his life. And he "loves" Idi Amin?

We may not be able to match Kivengere for dramatic effect, but all of us have somebody we can't imagine loving. Sometimes it's the people we are closest to—a brother or sister, a mother or father, a friend who has wronged us. But John comes back to us with the same persistent standard:

Big idea #4: love for God demands love for others.

"We love because He first loved us. If anyone says, 'I love God,' yet hates his brother, he is a liar. For anyone who does not love his brother, whom he has seen, cannot love God, whom he has not seen. And He has given us this command: Whoever loves God must also love his brother" (1 John 4:19-21).

Reminder: Love will not sit on the same shelf with hate. One shoves the other off. *Shatter!* Love lives in love. Love breeds love. Hate is foreign to all that.

But what grabs my mind as much as anything else John wrote is this: "Anyone who does not love his brother, whom he has seen, cannot love God, whom he has not seen" (1 John 4:20).

I protest. *John, it's easier to love God, whom I've not seen! When I see someone, I see his weaknesses. That makes him harder to love.*

And yet, I realize, that very thought shows how little I practice unconditional love. If I love unconditionally, I love in spite of what I see, not because of what I see.

Too often I reserve my love for the lovely people. It's fun to love God. I love my friends, particularly when they say nice things about me. I love my wife; it's a mutual thing we have going.

I sort people into categories—easy to love, hard to love, fun to love, impossible to love—all based on what I *see*. But when I do that, I am loving with reservations. I am holding back. My love is conditional.

And I suppose even my love for God carries its reservations, its conditional clauses. If I knew right now all God might permit me to someday endure, all the trials and sorrows, would it diminish my love for Him?

It may seem easier to love God, whom we've not seen. But that shows how little we understand the nature of unconditional love! And the command stands: "Whoever loves God must also love his brother" (1 John 4:21). That God gently points the way to His kind of love is further proof: *God can make life better.*

If Christianity is as great
as Christians say,
wouldn't you expect it
to be a joy, not a burden?
Where's the joy
in endless commands?

TEN

ETERNAL LIFE, ETERNAL SON
1 John 5:1-12

All I wanted was to know some *real* Christians. One man I once admired, a Sunday School teacher and church leader, had dumped his wife and family. Scratch one Christian example. Another church leader, whom I knew, was negative and sour. If Christianity did that to him, all I could say was, "Clear the area!"

The truth is, there were a few real Christians floating around; I recognize that now. But at the time, all I could see were the hypocrites. Still, I had a quiet hope that I would someday stumble across an authentic Christian.

During that unsettled time, my Christianity was a pit. It was a burden.

I would tell myself, "OK Self, let's love the creeps you can't stand." Self would not cooperate. "A little respect for parents maybe?" Slow going. "Alright Self, how about the filthy language? That *has* to change. What if the Christians find out about your mouth? Or the non-Christians about your faith?" And maybe I managed one week of clean talk.

Simply put, Christianity was a burden. And because it was such a colossal bother, something inside me began to die. I quit trying. I became inconsistent just like the hypocrite who dumped his family, or the sour church leader. Then, at that point of weakness, something happened.

Introducing the Truth

"Everyone who believes that Jesus is the Christ is born of God, and everyone who loves the Father loves his child as well" (1 John 5:1).

Some arguments you just can't tear down. And the greatest of these is love.

For me, the inarguable evidence that Christianity was true came in the form of a young couple I met. I've written about them before. And they made two things quite clear: (1) They loved God, and (2) they loved me. They showed me, by putting me on the receiving end of their example, that love for God expresses itself in love for people.

That flow of love is at the core of Christianity. *Our faith leads to Christ.* We believe He is who He claimed to be. We are born into God's family. Then *that same faith leads to love.*

"A new commandment I give you," Jesus told His disciples the night before His death. "Love one another. As I have loved you, so you must love one an-

```
        OBEY GOD   LOVE OTHERS
              LOVE GOD
```

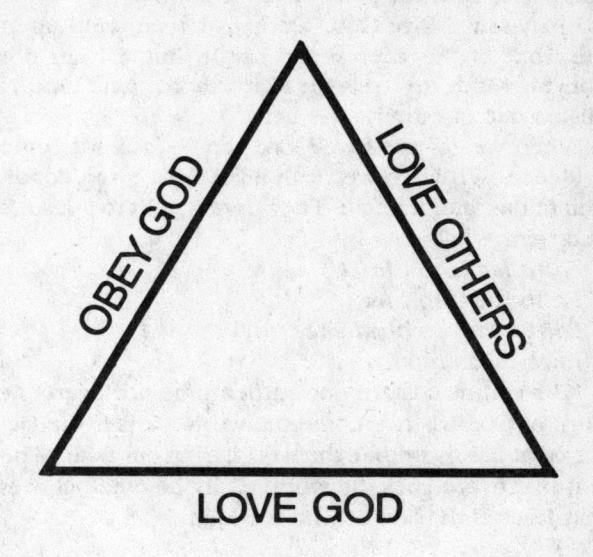

other. All men will know that you are My disciples if you love one another" (John 13:34-35).

Love shouts that our faith is real.

Faith leads to Christ.

Faith leads to love. And...

faith leads to obedience.

"This is how we know that we love the children of God: by loving God and carrying out His commands. This is love for God: to obey His commands" (1 John 5:2-3).

Imagine John constructing a triangle. On the base line he puts: *Love God*. On the other two lines he puts: *Obey God* and *Love Others*. Real Christianity consists of all three parts of this faith triangle.

I may say, "I love God." Perhaps I even stand up in the front of the church and say it. But if I am not obeying God, my triangle is fractured. One side is busted out and the base is bent.

When we say we love God, people look for some evidence. What are we really like? What's the condition of our faith triangle? They have a right to ask such questions.

Faith leads to Christ.
Faith leads to love.
Faith leads to obedience. And...
faith leads to victory.

"His commands are not burdensome, for everyone born of God has overcome the world. This is the victory that has overcome the world, even our faith. Who is it that overcomes the world? Only he who believes that Jesus is the Son of God" (1 John 5:3-5).

Beast of a Burden

Christianity makes such bold statements, such high demands. Take John's letters for example. His concepts are so clear-cut, so easily understood, so frustratingly straightforward.

"Anyone who claims to be in the light but hates his brother is still in darkness. Whoever loves his brother lives in the light, and there is nothing in him to make him stumble" (1 John 2:9-10).

John does not waste words. He's direct. And he does not waste space apologizing because the standard seems so high.

Check this one for example: "Do not love the world or anything in the world. If anyone loves the world, the love of the Father is not in him" (1 John 2:15).

Any question what John means? No question. Just high standards.

"No one who is born of God will continue to sin, because God's seed remains in him; he cannot go on sinning, because he has been born of God" (1 John 3:9).

In the midst of such impossible standards, such unattainable demands, John says, "His commands are not burdensome" (1 John 5:3). He does not say, "now give me a minute to explain this seeming inconsistency. What I really mean is..."

It would be tempting to look for a back door out of a verse like this, some way to explain it away. But truth is more tenacious than that. Toss it out the back door and you'll find it on your front porch.

What's John telling us? When Christ's love fills us, something happens to our outlook. Our attitudes shift. We look at the impossible standards and what do we see? *Love laws* designed for our good. They may not be breezy, but neither are they a burden. They are a discipline of joy.

That attitude shift, from burden to joy, is also tied in with the victory celebration. Through faith in Christ, we have overcome the world.

The world?

"Everything in the world—the cravings of sinful man, the lust of his eyes and the boasting of what he has and does—comes not from the Father but from the world. The world and its desires pass away, but the man who does the will of God lives forever" (1 John

2:16-17). *We overcome.*

The world?

"You, dear children, are from God and have overcome them, [the antichrists], because the One who is in you is greater than the one who is in the world" (1 John 4:4). *Open hostility does not better us.*

The world?

"In Me you may have peace. In this world you will have trouble. But take heart! I have overcome the world" (John 16:33). *Trouble needn't drag us down.*

Remember the faith triangle: *Love God, Obey God, Love Others.* It's a winning combination.

Triangle Two

When I was a college student, some weirdo mail-order religion got ahold of my name. And they did with it what most mail-order enterprises do: they mailed me a packet of junk, some junk mail.

I looked at the 8½" × 11" envelope and saw the name of a "church." Suspicious, I tore it open. Inside was an ordination certificate! All I had to do was sign it and send the postal church 10 buckolas and the State of California would authorize me, through this "church," to marry and bury.

And what did the mail order church believe? Anything. Build your own religion, a do-it-yourself special. Start with your basic basement beliefs. Add a few pillars of practice. Finish it off with some doctrinal dry wall. Believe anything you want. *Anything.*

That's a handy idea if you figure God's commands are burdensome. On the other hand, you could build the Christian way—and accept the teachings of the Bible.

Speaking of the Bible, I used to wonder why it has so much *history* in it. Why all the attention to factual details? Why not merely give the ideas, the concepts, the teachings? What's the point in all that history?

The point is, Christianity is tied to history, inseparably linked to *facts*. It is not some mystical mumbo-jumbo dreamed up by a spacy guru. Nor is it a philosophy noodled out by some scholar. Christianity is tied to events that really happened:

God created.

He led Israel out of Egypt.

He established David as king.

He brought Israel back from captivity.

He sent His Son.

He voiced His approval at His Son's baptism.

Death.

Burial.

Resurrection.

Events that really happened.

John says, "This is the One who came by water and blood—Jesus Christ. He did not come by water only, but by water and blood. And it is the Spirit who testifies, because the Spirit is the truth. For there are three that testify: the Spirit, the water, and the blood; and the three are in agreement" (1 John 5:6-8).

Water and blood. What do they say about Jesus? For one thing, they speak of a real death. John, the only disciple to witness the crucifixion of Jesus, made special note of water and blood. When one of the soldiers pierced Jesus' side with a spear, it brought a sudden flow of blood and water (John 19:34). Speaking of

```
        /\
       /  \
      /    \
     /WATER \BLOOD
    /        \
   /          \
  /_____\
      SPIRIT
```

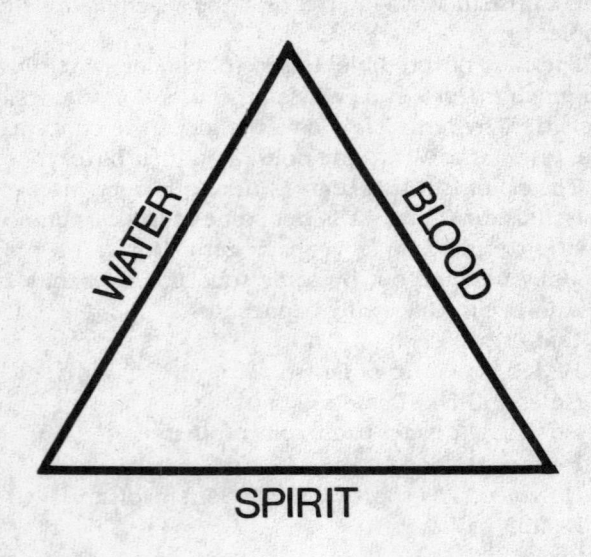

himself, John says: "The man who saw it [the water and blood flowing from Jesus' side] has given testimony, and his testimony is true. He knows that he tells the truth, and he testifies so that you also may believe" (John 19:35). The man Jesus really died.

But I think John is making another point as well. The false teachers, the antichrists, were teaching that "godness" came on Christ at His baptism. But three years later, when the going got rough, "godness" left Him. So it wasn't the *Christ* who died on the cross, only the *man* Jesus, the false teachers claimed.

But John says, "He did not come by water only, but by water and blood" (1 John 5:6). Jesus, the eternal God, did begin His public ministry at His baptism. But

His ministry reached its fulfillment with His sacrifice on the cross—"by water *and* blood."

The water and the blood are two reasons to trust Jesus, to accept Him as Lord. The third reason is the Holy Spirit. The Spirit speaks through the Bible and to us individually. And He says that Jesus is the Son of God, that we can believe in and rely on Him.

These three "reasons to believe" form a triangle—water, blood, and Spirit. The triangle cannot be broken without destroying Christianity itself.

"There are three that testify: the Spirit, the water, and the blood; and the three are in agreement" (1 John 5:7-8).

Who Can You Believe?

When I was a child I had an ornery streak. I often got in trouble at school. But one thing I rarely did: I rarely lied.

I remember how it hurt me to be confronted by my fifth-grade teacher and the principal and be accused of something I hadn't done. I told them I didn't do it. But the more I pled not guilty, the more they doubted and accused.

The incident is insignificant, but I remember the *feeling* of being doubted. The anger, disappointment, frustration. And what can a fifth-grade kid do to get his teacher and principal to listen?

Now I see people doubting God, rejecting what He has told us, and I want to scream: "Don't you know what it feels like to be doubted, to be called a liar? At

130 / New and Improved

> 1 John says:
> "God has given us eternal life, and this life is in His Son.
> He who has the Son has life;
> he who does not have the Son of God does not have life."
>
> That makes for a pretty clear choice, I guess.

least stop and listen!"

"We accept man's testimony, but God's testimony is greater because it is the testimony of God, which He has given about His Son. Anyone who believes in the Son of God has this testimony in his heart. Anyone who does not believe God has made Him out to be a liar, because he has not believed the testimony God has given about His Son" (1 John 5:9-10).

When you think of all that's involved, it is such an amazing courtesy that God bothers to offer us any explanations at all. He's not like some troublemaking kid being accused of something he didn't do. He's more like the principal offering forgiveness, only to have some brat spit on his shoe.

"And this is the testimony: God has given us eternal life, and this life is in His Son. He who has the Son has life; he who does not have the Son of God does not have life" (1 John 5:11-12)

Most people don't like to hear about hell. The idea of eternal punishment is certainly not vogue party talk.

But John wants us to listen in on God's perspective, to find out how He views life and death, heaven and hell. So John dials His number, then leaves the phone off the hook. We pick up the receiver and press it to our ear as God shares candidly:

Not accepting the testimony—that Jesus is God's Son—is rejecting. Refusing the truth is calling God a liar. There is an outer limit of grace; step beyond that point and you find yourself falling.

You whirl around and look above you. But everything that ever made you feel secure is terrifyingly out of reach. You are rushing away from it at an incredible speed, plummeting into an abyss of eternal death. You look into the face of Christ, far, far above you, and what you see destroys you.

He's crying.

Discovery.
There's a certain brand
of enthusiasm
reserved for people
who find things out
and are glad.
Big things.
Significant things.
Hard-to-explain things.

ELEVEN

GOD HEARS, GOD ANSWERS
1 John 5:13-21

From the living room sofa, I could look out across Manhattan Beach to the endless expanse of the Pacific Ocean. There was, and is, an awesomeness about that view of sky and sea. The sea becomes for me a symbol of something far greater. Each swell that curls and breaks, the continuous ebb and flow; it's all part of a bigger picture with special meaning. I have always thought of the sea as one of the great natural analogies of God. Boundless. Powerful. At once comforting and threatening.

Southern California's Manhattan Beach has special significance to me because of the time I spent there at the end of my senior year of high school, and the two summers that followed. That time, when I was involved in evangelism, solidified my commitment.

So when I say that, for me, the sea is an analogy of God and His work, I'm not just being poetic. At Manhattan Beach those three summers the analogy and the reality were brought together, placed side by side for me to consider.

I would rise early in the morning, grab my Bible, and walk across the sand, almost close enough to the surf to feel its spray. In that solitude, I would read and pray.

If I felt I wasn't quite getting through to God, I would walk along the beach, praying aloud. I would scan the horizon and toss my questions to God, as if the receding tide carried them to Him for me. And I would imagine God sending His love back in return. I would visualize it, like the waves washing driftwood ashore.

Later in the day, there on the beach, my friends and I would talk to children, young people, and adults about Christianity. We'd walk along the pier and strike up conversations with people who had nothing to do but soak up the sun and think.

I learned a little bit about listening. I understood some of the frustrations people were carrying. I struggled through the questions that they raised. Again and again I felt my powerlessness. I would share the Gospel, and it would be met with reluctance, hesitation. I wanted to reach out and make the decisions for people, not just because I believed it all, but because something was happening to me those weeks. Christianity was becoming more beautiful.

How can I explain it? It was like, before that time, I believed Christianity was true; now I also *felt* that truth. It was like, before, Jesus Christ was a part of me, but now I was a part of Him. And I wanted to share the news: *God can make life better!*

I stood out on the end of the pier one blustery afternoon, and I looked straight down at the currents swirling around the pilings. Then I looked out across the blue-green expanse. But instead of feeling small and insignificant, I felt extremely important. Valued. Loved. In all of this vastness, the Creator knew *me*, cared for me, understood me, accepted me. I was a friend of the Creator's Son.

I wanted to grab the person next to me and ask, "How does all this vastness make you feel? Have you thought about God today?" But I figured he'd peg me a lunatic, so I restrained myself. Besides, not everyone reacts to vastness in the same way.

Some people, looking at the same scene, would perceive blue sky, blue sea, salt air, but nothing more. Vastness? How philosophical.

Someone else would feel the vastness, but figure that's all there was. Why assume there is a vast Creator just because "creation" is so vast?

Other people would sense the vastness and feel uneasy, perhaps even scared. They would accurately perceive their smallness, perhaps even God's bigness, but then what? Where does that lead? I've talked with people who fear God but will not accept the idea that His love can cast that fear into the drink.

Manhattan Beach reminded me that you can ignore God, or you can run from Him in fear. Or you can turn to Him in faith. But if you come to Him, you must come on His terms. You can't tame the sea.

The average person doesn't absorb all that. Creation may give him hints about God (Romans 1:20), but God has given Christians the awesome responsibility of explaining those clues.

Before Inverting the World . . .

Christians are people with the job of turning the world upside down, sharing the discovery: *God can make life better.* But world-inverting is an ambitious task. If we're not quite sure which side of the world *we* are on, it's dangerous to try to flip it around. Before sharing the discovery, we need to be sure of our own condition.

John stresses the point: "I write these things to you who believe in the name of the Son of God so that you may know that you have eternal life" (1 John 5:13).

Feel free to tack on: *not hope, not think, but know!* But to add that phrase, we must first be sure we understand "these things."

John writes this entire letter, 1 John, with a clear purpose in mind, just as he did with his Gospel. John's Gospel concludes with, "These are written that you may believe that Jesus is the Christ, the Son of God, and that by believing you may have life in His name" (John 20:30-31). John wrote his Gospel *that we might believe in Christ.*

As he brings this letter to a close, John says that he wrote it *to assure us in our belief.* He wants us to have confidence about our relationship with God.

But the assurance John offers is not unconditional. We can't live a gunky life and then rejoice in "assurance of salvation."

What is the basis of our assurance? It is that we have tested our lives against the principles of 1 John and have found that Jesus Christ has changed us. Not that we are perfect, but we are better.

We walk in the light.

We confess sin.
We obey His commands.
We love our brothers.
We do not love the world.
We are not swayed by false teachers.
We continue in Christ.
We do not wallow in sin.
We believe that Jesus is the Christ, God's sent Son.

When your own life is upright and you know it, you can tell when something needs to be inverted.

Talking Terms

It takes power to turn the world upside down. And John tells us: "This is the assurance we have in approaching God: that if we ask anything according to His will, He hears us. And if we know that He hears us—whatever we ask—we know that we have what we asked of Him" (1 John 5:14-15).

This is John's fourth discussion of *boldness*. Two passages refer to boldness and judgment, and two passages, this one and another, refer to boldness in prayer.

We can look forward to Christ's return with confidence if we preserve the closeness of our relationship with Him (1 John 2:28). If we have God's love working in our lives, we are *like God*. We don't have to be afraid of being judged. We can be bold before Him (1 John 4:17-18).

The joy of loving obedience also produces the joy of a clean conscience, the freedom to ask God *anything*. "Dear friends, if our hearts do not condemn us, we have confidence before God and receive from Him anything we ask, because we obey His commands and do what pleases Him" (1 John 3:21).

If we ask according to His will, He *hears* us (1 John 5:14). And if He *hears*, He will *answer* (v. 15).

It's almost funny to think of Almighty God listening to us. "He sits enthroned above the circle of the earth, and its people are like grasshoppers. He stretches out the heavens like a canopy, and spreads them out like a tent to live in. He brings princes to naught and reduces the rulers of this world to nothing" (Isaiah 40:22-23). Yet John says, "If we ask anything according to His will He hears us" (1 John 5:14).

In spite of that assurance, most Christians have problems with prayer. We pray prayers that aren't answered. And when that happens, we tend to lose interest. Prayer becomes a meaningless religious duty.

Question: Why don't prayers get answered? World-inverters need to know!

How about *wrong motives in asking?* James warns: "You do not have, because you do not ask God. When you ask, you do not receive, because you ask with wrong motives, that you may spend what you get on your pleasures" (James 4:2-3). In other words, sometimes we pray selfishly.

How about unconfessed sin? "If I had cherished sin in my heart, the Lord would not have listened" (Psalm 66:18). *Sin hinders prayer.*

Perhaps the main reason prayers go begging for answers is more basic. Prayers don't get the answers we're hunting for because *we ask for the wrong things.* When the Bible adds the phrase, "ask anything according to His will" (1 John 5:14), it's not to give the Lord an escape clause in case we ask something too hard. That statement is there because people are likely to ask for the wrong things.

Why? Sometimes we are just boxed in by our own human limitations. Other times we are careless. Often we are preoccupied with things of secondary importance. If we were to make a list of our prayer requests, and after a month compare them with the prayers of the Bible, most of us would be hard-pressed to find much similarity.

What's Important?

John gives an example of the kind of thing that should be a prayer-priority for world-inverters: the spiritual health of our Christian brothers and sisters. "If anyone sees his brother commit a sin that does not lead to death, he should pray and God will give him life. I refer to those whose sin does not lead to death. There is a sin that leads to death. I am not saying that he should pray about that. All wrongdoing is sin, and there is sin that does not lead to death" (1 John 5:16-17).

I wonder if John realized the controversy he would stir by bringing up "sin that leads to death"? Some Christians are eager to identify one specific sin so they can avoid that one sin only.

Problem is, "sin that leads to death" is apparently not any one particular sin, but rather continuing in sin that hurts the reputation of the church. Ananias and Sapphira, the deceitful duo of the early church, lied to the apostles and to the Holy Spirit and woke up dead (Acts 5:1-11). People in Corinth were sickly or "slept"—permanently—because of sin they refused to make right (1 Corinthians 11:30).

We are to pray for our brothers and sisters who are involved in sin, but we are not to pray for those who are caught in a sin that leads to death. So how do we know when to pray and when not to? Sounds funny, but if they die, don't bother to pray for them. That's not as strange as it sounds. Some religious groups pray for the dead constantly. Christianity says, "The time to pray is now."

Getting back to prayer-priorities, if my fellow Christian has not committed sin that leads to death, *How do I pray for him? What do I ask?*

Consider: "We have not stopped praying for you," Paul said of the Colossians, "and asking God to fill you with the knowledge of His will through all spiritual wisdom and understanding. And we pray this in order that you may live a life worthy of the Lord and may please Him in every way: bearing fruit in every good work, growing in the knowledge of God, being strengthened with all power according to His glorious might so that you may have great endurance and patience" (Colossians 1:9-11).

Double-check that list. Compare Paul's prayer concerns with your own.

If we prayed regularly for our fellow Christians, using Paul's requests as a model, we'd all be in better spiritual health. God would answer. The world would seem lighter, more easily inverted.

We need spiritual wisdom and understanding more than we need an A in French. We need endurance and patience more than we need to shake the flu. We need to learn what to ask for in prayer.

Parting Shot

John concludes his letter by reviewing three things that we Christians know, three things that equip us to turn the world upside down.

We know #1: Christians must live morally. "We know that anyone born of God does not continue to sin; the One who was born of God keeps him safe, and the evil one does not touch him" (1 John 5:18).

When John discussed this issue on an earlier orbit, he stressed that Christians do not continue in a life of sin, because they are born of God. They have new life. Now he hints at the active work of Jesus Christ preserving us, lifting us up, and keeping us.

We know #2: Christians belong to God. "We know that we are children of God, and that the whole world is under the control of the evil one" (1 John 5:19).

The world system has great power. Behind the scenes, Satan controls it. But neither the world nor Satan have authority over true Christians.

For centuries Christians have ached and strained, trying to turn the world upside down. It's an unending task. But one way or another, sooner or later, it has to happen.

"Then the end will come, when He [Christ] hands over the kingdom to God the Father after He has destroyed all dominion, authority, and power" (1 Corinthians 15:24).

The world will be inverted. No question. Right now, Christians have the amazing privilege of inviting people to find the better life God offers, and to avoid the consequences of refusing Him.

We know #3: Christians have the understanding

they need. "We know also that the Son of God has come and has given us understanding, so that we may know Him who is true. And we are in Him who is true—even in His Son Jesus Christ. He is the true God and eternal life" (1 John 5:20).

The false teachers enjoyed talking about eternal life and "knowing God the Father." But they excluded Jesus; they ignored His claim of being God's sent Son. John said that if you set Jesus aside, you set eternal life aside.

The false teachers liked to talk of God as "the Father." But Jesus said, "If anyone loves Me, he will obey My teaching. My Father will love him, and We will come to him and make Our home with him" (John 14:23).

That's why John concludes his letter by saying: "Dear children, keep yourselves from idols" (1 John 5:21).

What is an idol, but a false concept of God? John had to contend with the antichrists whose false concept was to favor God the Father and reduce Jesus to a commonplace man—nice teachings, good life, but not God.

Today people are strapped with similar, twisted ideas of who God is, what He's like. The wrong ideas need to be overturned. Lovingly inverted.

Which brings me back to a conversation in a parking lot with a preacher friend. It wasn't a dramatic sermon, just a quiet comment: "One person, who really believed God, could turn this city upside down." When he said that, I realized that I wanted to be such a person. Six months later, I was on Manhattan Beach, beginning to learn what it means to be a world-inverter.

I think of the vastness of that Pacific Ocean and

remember, as insignificant as I sometimes feel, I am extremely important. Valued. Loved. In all that vastness, the Creator knows me, cares for me, understands me, accepts me. He is the boundless, powerful resource I need to invert my world. But He is also the personal, caring friend I need to sort out life's questions.

You can't hog a discovery like that. It has to be shared: God can make life better!